Other Books by Dave Pelzer

A Child Called "It"

The Lost Boy

A Man Named Dave

Help Yourself

The Privilege of Youth

Help Yourself for Teens

Moving Forward

TOO CLOSE TO ME

The Middle-Aged Consequences of Revealing *A Child Called "It"*

DAVE PELZER

New York, 2015

First edition published 2015 by RosettaBooks
Cover design by David Ter-Avanesyan / Ter33Design
Interior design by Alexia Garaventa
Jacket photo by Macbrian Mun / Moment Open / Getty Images

Library of Congress Control Number: 2014958836

ISBN-13: *978-0-7953-51273*

www.RosettaBooks.com

Printed in the United States of America

DEDICATION & IN MEMORIAM

To my *B*— my lovely, pure of heart, reassuring, comical, most gentlest soul I know, my bride, Kay, who saved me from myself and for good or ill, simply allows me to be me!!!

In loving memory of Athena Konstan, an extraordinary woman and passionate educator, who for well over thirty-five years challenged her students to greatness, all the while living the adventure of a grand life!!!

In loving memory of Jacqueline Howard, who was the Mrs. Cleaver of Dunsmuir Way. Thank you for being everyone's mom.

CONTENTS

ACKNOWLEDGMENTS

This was an extraordinary, gargantuan endeavor—over nine years in the making. While trying to fathom and come to terms with yet another monumental failure in my life, and while simultaneously obtusely putting myself at extreme risk on the far sides of thc world, I attempted to write about the experiences that I brought upon myself.

When completed, the word count was over 178,000—the average tome being around 60,000. So, needless to say, I had to go back and not simply trim the fat, but truly rethink and restructure the entire tone of the book.

For me, I'd rather be in the middle of harm's way than face the grinding descaling process of a massive rewrite, which I dubbed "Project 9."

With that confession, I humbly thank editors Elizabeth Stein, for helping me attempt to go around the Horn of Africa in the worst of conditions when it became Book 8, and Emilie Jackson, who helped pilot Project 9 through the still channels of the Panama Canal. I thank you ladies for your tremendous skill and astute dedication.

I also am grateful to my longtime agent and dear friend Laurie Liss for her patience and guidance with me in the New World of publishing.

Lastly, I am truly indebted to the director of my offices, Kathryn Larkin-Estey, who depending upon the conditions of our hypersonic-filled days, I lovingly dub "Mrs. C" or simply "M"—the hard-nosed, no-nonsense yet maternal boss who not only protects but warns her operatives of the serious nature of their missions' true intentions. I can never thank you enough for ALL our endless meetings, your precious time, and putting up with me while I examine and break down complicated situations to the minutest meaning in order to better understand how to proceed in my various crusades.

SPECIAL NOTES

Some of the names have been changed in order to protect the privacy and dignity of others.

As with the books *A Child Called "It," The Lost Boy, A Man Named Dave,* and *The Privilege of Youth*, in my mind's eye, I've always had a musical thread, a unique song that related to the core of each of these stories. I've been blessed to incorporate and draw from the exceptionally talented well of multi–Grammy Award–winning (twenty to date) Pat Metheny.

Because of the complexity of *Too Close to Me*, I've selected a trilogy of songs that best convey the texture of this book. For the first two acts, I've chosen Pat Metheny's "Polish Paths" and "A Change in Circumstance." And for the second half of Chapter 17, I selected Hans Zimmer's haunting piece entitled "Time."

PREFACE

This book is not what it initially appears to be.

It is not about yet another broken affair that appears on various tabloid shows on a seemingly hourly basis. And it is certainly not some salacious, tattletale tell-all tome.

This book is about relationships, both business and personal, and what we all bring into them. It is about the ramifications of our choices and our failure to take action in a large part because of our unresolved experiences.

It is a deep examination of one's life while questioning one's values and purpose during an unexpected midlife "fork in the road" crisis.

It is about how some of us, stupidly, even arrogantly, keep repeating lifelong patterns while plowing ahead, placing a great deal at risk, while attempting to repair whatever situation, in the mere hope that one's efforts will yield some new, transformed result.

On a deeper level, this book is also about our subconscious fears and demons and the devastating effect they can have on the decisions of our lives in the "real world."

Yet, at the core, this book is about coming to terms and putting down some of the weight of our own crosses that, as middle-aged adults, we all seem to bear. It is about how every day is another chance, another opportunity to achieve happiness and the empowerment of forgiveness. It is about giving ourselves permission to acknowledge our worth and to allow goodness into the remainder of our days.

This book is about the acceptance of grace that we all deserve.

CHAPTER 1

THE RUNNING MAN

I'VE ALWAYS BEEN A RUNNER. I've always been in some frantic hurry, struggling to stave off an inevitable confrontational situation, or trying to split the atoms of time so I could not only meet and accomplish all objectives, but simultaneously fight to shave corners, to carve out time in the hope of being able to lower my shield in order to feel safe.

As a small child, I was trained to perform an endless list of chores with impossible time requirements, with scraps of food as my possible reward. My perpetrator mother would command me with a snap of her fingers, and if I did not move fast enough to stand exactly three feet in front of her, with my chin locked down to my chest and my hands glued to my side, I was assaulted without mercy.

I would sit on top of my hands for hours at a time, either at the bottom of the darkened stairs of the basement or on piles of rocks outside in the fog-filled backyard, my mind racing. I would formulate ideas to ease the throbbing pain or come up with seemingly over-the-top schemes to steal food.

As I ran to school every morning with my tattered long-sleeved shirt flapping in every direction, I'd pump my pencil-sized arms and stretch my legs to gain speed, hoping to snatch pieces of food from inside the treasure-filled metal lunch boxes of my classmates before school started.

Later, at age twelve, after I had been rescued and placed in protective foster care, my spindly legs and my bursts of speed helped keep me at arm's length from the roaming packs of hardened schoolyard bullies.

And even though I was finally safe from the constant torture, dungeon-like isolation, and degrading humiliation, I still did all I could to flee from the slime of my past. Fragments of my history bubbled to the surface, penetrating my hardwired black-and-white sphere of logic. My emotional side began to contemplate ways I could win the approval of my sick abuser.

As a young teen, while others explored their privileges of youth, I raced from job to job, putting in forty hours a week or more while in junior high and then as many as eighty hours while in high school. Terrified of being homeless and starving when the day eventually came that I departed foster care, I blazed to stay ahead of my peers who had the safety net of their loving families.

At the age of eighteen, I found my footing. I continued to push myself with a razor-sharp focus. I became tenacious when it came to my new ambition, enlisting with the air force. They, rightfully, had little interest in a stuttering, outwardly awkward high school dropout. Yet, even with little education, low admission test scores, and the stigma of coming from foster care, after six months of pestering the recruiters on a daily basis, I was finally allowed to sign up.

A few years later when a handful of specialized paramilitary slots became available, while others trained by trotting a few miles a week, I ran fifteen miles per session, several times a week, in boots. At the same time, I had to fight to deprogram myself and believe that I was worthy enough to attend a college class in basic algebra, and even though it took me three separate attempts, my drive made the difference.

The ultimate military marathon came in over two years' time. I had repeatedly applied for a coveted air crew member slot in which my substantial paperwork was either mishandled or lost time and again as my days of enlistment dwindled away. Yet through stubborn perseverance, I was fortunate enough to eventually land a position with the highly secretive SR-71 Blackbird spy plane.

As my divine dream of donning a flight suit began to take hold, I momentarily stopped to survey how lucky I truly was compared to others who seemed to be standing still, or (without their knowledge) slowly sliding into their own self-made sinkholes. My reflection instantly connected me to the guilt I carried over my brothers, who were left behind when I was removed, and how they were faring as young men making their own paths. My stillness also instantly reconnected me with the painful memories of my father, who literally stood over me when Mother made me swallow ammonia, only muttering about the possible need to "feed the boy so he won't steal any food." Then, years later, I stood over the former San Francisco firefighter, holding his hand and gently kissing him good-bye as he drew his last breath before passing away. Up until that very moment, I believed with childlike logic I could accomplish *something* that would somehow instantly repair years worth of suffering and damage.

It was during this time, in my early twenties, when I discovered that whenever I wasn't in some form of forward trajectory, an invisible lead blanket of shame seemed to cover me and suffocate my being. The strain of the immense weight and all it represented was too much for me to even begin to deal with.

A short time later I married the first girl I had a relationship with. We had a beautiful baby boy. For someone who carefully analyzed aeronautics, I paid little heed to interpersonal relationships. Whenever a marital crisis erupted and I felt my trust was violated, I was saved by jumping on a jet and flying away from my problems for months at a time.

But one day while at base housing, I didn't shy away from confrontation as I had countless times before. Across the street from me, I observed a young child being yelled at before being struck in public view. The shrill echo and raged-filled eyes of the child's mother reconnected me to my very own perpetrator.

In an instant, the event flipped a giant circuit breaker and changed my entire life. From the deepest part of me, I detested deliberate cruelty toward others. While others became upset, some saw red, even black. My recessed rage was pure molten white.

I was living the adventurous life of a secretive air crew member and had my loving, beautiful, blond-haired boy by my side, and even though I knew my marriage was sliding into an abyss, I felt I had been given so much.

Maybe too much.

I felt more than a mere need to assist, more than a knee-jerk reaction to help. For a plethora of deep-seated justifications—for my brothers, my broken father, my teachers who rescued me, my foster parents who guided me, the dedicated social workers, for anyone who kindly gave me the time of day, and even for my tormented mother and her then-unmentionable past, I *had* to step up and do something.

With the purest of intentions, I began a journey on an unexpected path. Over time it became an all-consuming mission, every free second of every day.

I couldn't run fast enough to keep up.

And beneath my internal shield where I hid even from God Himself, the Kryptonite of my past slowly killed me. The more I helped, the more I gave of myself, the more my life force spilled away like water circling down a sink's drain. My mission became a virus that fed off of my need to cleanse myself by doing even more. And it affected more than just me.

After decades of work that spanned the globe in my one-man, dragging-my-own-cross crusade, in the end, I only ended up coming full circle with the two specters that I had fled from for my entire life: my perpetrator, and the child called "It."

CHAPTER 2

JUSTIFIABLE DENIAL

I USED TO RUN SO WELL. I had rhythm, flow, and the strongest of hearts. I had an inner drive that could go on and on, and when I was depleted, I could still excel. My determination was endless. But it took a second failed marriage and a worsening medical situation that stemmed from my childhood for me to begin to stop racing and truly study the repercussions of my life's choices. Yet I felt changing my behavior was like trying to pull the lever to the brakes on a mile-long runaway locomotive.

For a multitude of reasons, or even justifications, I ran to remain as far away as possible from the filth and shame associated with my past. I didn't recognize then my *need* for perpetual motion. And after thirty-five years, my defensive habit morphed into a natural condition. From the inner recesses of my brain, I conditioned myself to believe if I kept moving forward, I could possibly create a clean barrier between me and my past.

Running became beneficial. I quickly found out that my ceaseless motion meant I was constantly "out there," helping others, and the more I was out there, the less time and energy I had to examine my side of the street, so to speak, and all of my peculiar internal issues.

When it came to assisting others, I was absolutely sincere. With a newborn son, I began to open my eyes to the world around me. I thought there was nothing more deplorable than to turn a blind eye on any helpless child being mistreated. I'm sure part of my process might have stemmed from the deep well of resentment I carried like a lead bucket from my former life, as Mother's prisoner. So many people knew of my situation, but for whatever reason or excuse, refused to intervene with even a simple word or kind gesture.

What began as a few hours a month with the county as a youth service worker turned into a part-time position in juvenile hall. It got to the point where I would land from a late-night mission with the air force, sprint to my car, drive hundreds of miles, and volunteer at some event early the next morning. In a short span of time, as I crisscrossed the entire state, the thrill from helping even more began to overtake me.

When I hung up my flight suit and became a civilian, I began to travel throughout the country, adding even more by giving hundreds of extensive certified presentations based on the concepts of resilience and self-reliance, no matter what one's past. By then, not including time at airports or sometimes driving throughout the evening, I was pulling in sixteen-hour workdays.

All the while, I longed to do something special for those who had intervened and saved my life. I wrote a series of long letters that I later combined into a book. I then proudly presented the actual first copies of my tome to my teachers on the very day of the twenty-year anniversary of my rescue.

As my crusade progressed even more, I was fortunate enough to receive several prestigious accolades. But it was twenty-four months after my first book was published (four years after it was initially printed), when it became a best seller, that I was suddenly labeled as *somebody*.

Then, all hell broke loose. With my newfound commercial success, I was constantly being pushed and pulled in every direction. I couldn't possibly do enough to satisfy all of the requests. At times, people demanded heaven and earth, and even proclaimed my past was an elaborate fabrication. It didn't matter that I had already been heavily vetted with top secret clearances by the air force and the highest offices for my awards, or that extensive interviews were held with my teachers and my foster parents. For some, my situation seemed too much to be true.

To me it seemed obvious and so simple to fix: by chasing after the approval from those who treated me the worst. Because of my high value of integrity, coupled with my sensitive ego, I actually fought to *defend* my validity. But the more I did this, the more I sank into a vast pit of quicksand. By then I was spending more than two hundred days a year on the road, often sleeping on the floors of airport terminals and surviving on cold, soggy fast food, my only reward for completing my duties for the day.

After a while the cycle seemed so normal.

After all, attempting to survive in the midst of chaos was engrained in me.

By the time I was eight, I had already been Mother's selected target for nearly four years. One sunny afternoon as I returned home from school, I found Mother, who had been alone all day, in her typical foul mood, but worse. After a few rants and slaps, she went on to state how I had made her life a living hell and how she had planned to show me "what hell is all about."

After burning my arm just above the gas stove, Mother went on to inform me that because of the pain I had caused her, she intended to make me to lie down on the gas stove and burn for her. Terrified as never before, and facing the reality that we were alone and she could do with me as she pleased, out of raw, desperate fear, I came up with a plan to stall Mother and prevent her from burning me further. As commanded, I would stand up, but rather than take one second to do so, I'd fumble and take four seconds or more. Then, instead of standing exactly three feet in front of her, I'd stand a few steps farther away, just out of striking distance. It meant receiving slaps, punches, and kicks, but it was a small price to offset the alternative.

For the very first time in my life, and after years of being completely conditioned like Pavlov's dog, I thought for myself and developed my own form of control.

Afterward, alone in the darkened basement where Mother allowed me to reside, the shock of the episode subsided and I inspected my latest injury. I then foolishly licked my blistered arm, which immediately gave me the sensation of jamming my finger in a light socket. But as I wept from another form of pain, I realized that if I could feel, I was alive, I had made it. And, through my own actions, I had stopped my perpetrator from her sickening evil plan—I had done it.

From above, I could hear Mother coo to my eldest brother, Ron, how immensely proud she was of *him*. In a flash, I realized that I was not the demon child that Mother had brainwashed me into believing since before my days in kindergarten. I was not the sole reason Mother was so unhappy. As a small child, I had sensed that something was wrong. But as I examined my bubbled blisters, I came to understand that that *something* was not me.

It was then that I became conscious of the seriousness of my escalating situation. I finally came to accept that it was becoming increasingly bizarre and gruesome. It was out of fear and sheer desperation that I had to determine my fate on my own terms. I could either continue to remain passive, hoping and praying that things just might suddenly change, or I could try to do something, anything, for my well-being. I could try. I could do it for me.

Alone at the bottom of the basement stairs, with tears in my eyes, I stood up and raised my arm in a pledge. If I could change the equation and continue to accomplish what I just had, then I could, I *would*, do anything possible in order to survive. That afternoon, with Almighty God as my witness, I vowed that I would never cave, and from that moment on I would do anything I could in order to survive.

My zealous oath, which literally saved my skin countless times as Mother's prisoner and then later throughout my life, catapulted me beyond any unimaginable dream, but this came at an immense cost.

At times I felt shut out. Or in a flash, out of panic or resentment, I would shut down. I had grave issues with trust, let alone getting close to anyone beyond my own son. And above all things, I felt I had to remain constantly vigilant.

This all fed into my continued need to remain on the run.

And then as a man well into my forties and having been on my crusade for nearly two decades, all I had to show for it was yet another failed relationship.

Sitting in the expansive living room, I noticed how still the house had become. For the first time since moving from Northern California, there was no screeching echo from Marsha's exotic bird, no endless high-pitched barking from her three overly hyper bichon dogs, none of the personal drama of me fighting to solve yet another financial blunder caused by my wife's continual shopping sprees.

After our tumultuous times as husband and wife, as well as the high-strung intensity of trying to work together, I thought that with Marsha gone, *all* of my problems would have naturally fled with her.

I was alone.

Beginning to reflect, I took in a deep, clean breath. While slowly massaging my throat, I thought maybe now was the time to finally stop and take inventory of my deep-rooted beliefs.

I felt the boa constrictor—like tension around my throat begin to ease. As I stretched it further by leaning backward, I closed my eyes. I could hear the faint rush of air suddenly escape my larynx. Overwhelmed and tired, I felt myself become overtaken with sleep.

From the far side of the house, I heard a deep creaking noise. In a flash, my internal hyperattentive radar was reactivated. The sound itself instantly set off one of my primal triggers.

One Sunday after the burn incident, Mother announced to me in front of my spiritually broken, passive father that because I was so much trouble for her, I no longer deserved to be a member of the family. She spewed out a stream of new rules, including my no longer being allowed to make eye contact with her, my father, or my siblings, my name never to be mentioned, and my new sleeping quarters to be next to the kitty litter box under the kitchen table. I was also commanded to perform even more chores, and then when finished, I was to stand for hours on end at the far side of the entrance to the garage.

After learning to adjust to my new area, I found an old wooden ladder and would lean against it to rest from the mental and physical exhaustion. Since I was beneath the house, I quickly learned to filter and distinguish every form of noise from above, my body snapping to alert whenever I thought the upstairs door opened.

One evening after a draining week of performing chores and receiving little to no leftover food as my reward, I listened to The Family upstairs as they gorged themselves on one of Mother's fantastic homemade dinners. I escaped my misery by closing my eyes and fantasizing that I was worthy enough to sit at the dinner table and enjoy a real meal.

I must have fallen asleep. When I awoke, I no longer heard the laughter or the clanging of utensils from above. What I did hear was the unique stomping of Mother's heavy feet as she marched down the short hallway and then into the bathroom where she turned the squeaking knob to fill the bathtub.

Directly above me I could hear the sudden rush of water running through the pipes. To be sure of my safety, I turned to the left and looked up toward the basement stairs. As if on cue, I saw the filtered light from Mother opening the door. She then flipped on the switch to the downstairs light before she made her way down the set of steps.

Immediately, as I had been trained over the years, I reverted to the "position of address": my arms glued to the sides of my legs, my head bent down to my upper chest, and my eyes locked to the cement floor.

My pulse quickened as I fought to control my breathing. As I closed my eyes, I counted the amount of steps and timed them. I then imagined Mother opening the door to my brothers' downstairs bedroom and then going through the various bureau drawers to retrieve fresh pajamas for them.

Usually the entire sequence would last three to four minutes, ending with Mother slamming the upstairs door, representative of her hatred for me. But because I let down my guard, distracted by the pipes' vibrating sounds from the water leading into the bathroom, I became frightened that I might have missed my cue.

After five minutes of counting backward from sixty at a snail's pace, I still failed to hear Mother's slamming of the door. Drawing in another breath, I slowly counted backward for another minute. But as I did, my tension took over. I cheated. Ever so slowly, I strained my ears for any clue. Then, by the smallest of fractions, I raised my throbbing chin, while at the same time turning it up and to the left. As I did, my eyes adjusted and I could make out the wooden rail of the staircase. Thankfully the light was off, meaning Mother must have already gone upstairs.

I almost smiled. But something didn't feel right. I felt an odd coldness surround me. As I continued to swivel my head farther to the left, I could make out, just behind me, on the right side of my back, Mother standing.

The shock of seeing her standing so close to me with the piercing gaze of hate in her eyes made me urinate on myself. I quickly reverted back to my position. All the while I could hear her slow, labored breathing. After a few additional minutes, unsure if I had imagined the experience, I dared to look again.

She was indeed behind me, only closer.

Without a word, Mother simply leaned against me, as if she were a snake about to strike with its venomous fangs. I clamped my eyes as tight as possible. Beginning to shake, I could feel more warm fluid spill down my rattling legs. Somehow, through my submissive fear, I knew I was inviting Mother to attack. All I could do was try to remain in position.

In my hyperpaced brain, I counted backward over and over, in various sets of sequences. Suddenly I heard the water from above me turn off and the muffled, reverberating sounds of Mother walking out of the bathroom and into the kitchen, where she began to run down my father in her distinctive, chilling tone. Only then did I open my eyes. I had no idea when she left. And to be absolutely sure, I didn't dare move a hair.

From that moment on, I promised myself I'd never again let down my guard. Even when I became cold from the Bay Area fog that seeped through the mail slot where I stood, I didn't move a millimeter from the "position of address." Or, no matter how drained I was from performing my endless chores, I didn't dare close my eyes, let alone find comfort by leaning on the ladder.

The cost of getting caught, or even being remotely vulnerable, was simply too high.

As an adult, sitting alone in my house after the sensation of being startled had passed, I thought again about my "running" issues. And, like a million times before, I justified to myself that after my latest scare, *now* was not the time.

CHAPTER 3

THE CONSTANT GARDENER

FOR ME, STILLNESS WAS AN ISSUE. Yet, as much as I ran through my life's ambitious marathons and pushed myself well beyond the normal limits, I felt I still had even more to do. To be alone with nothing to accomplish, with only my own thoughts, was tantamount to being sealed alive in a coffin.

Even back when Marsha would fly out to visit her family back east, because of her pets, I was never alone and the house was never still. With my wife and her drama and her animals gone, the house became serene. But still I did not feel safe.

Late into the night, unable to rest, and feeling insecure in my new setting, I rearranged a few items in the living room. I then quickly found myself going in full force, doing the same throughout the entire house.

I had just flown home that very afternoon from being on the road. Marsha had fled the day before in a private transport, and the house felt like a spring-loaded trap ready to snap. Before I even drove back to the house, I broke from my own strict regimen and went on a spontaneous shopping spree. I felt the urge to sanitize after my failure. I splurged on sheets, pillowcases, and a duvet cover for the bedroom; a new coffee maker for the kitchen; and for the rest of the house, scented candles and oil diffusers of various sizes and colors.

Upon first moving into the house, and thinking of how it would make my wife happy, every item and piece of furniture was selected by her. Yet it seemed every time I returned from the road, entire rooms of the house were completely redone. It didn't seem to matter that an expensive couch was not even a month old. If something suddenly caught Marsha's eye, be it in the middle of a showroom floor or in her daily stacks of specialty magazines, she would instantly pounce and replace some "older" item in our home.

I couldn't help but recall just a few months ago when Marsha had our bed covered with a combination of bright purple, orange, and black Versace bed linens with enormous pillow shams to match. She loved the ultraluxurious designer fashions, but the whole color combination made my head spin. And, no matter how I pried, I never found out how much the gaudy extravagance had cost.

Earlier that day while I volunteered at an upscale fundraiser on Rodeo Drive, Marsha, with cumulating bags in hand, scurried up and down the road, visiting the famed shops. From deep within, I fought to swallow my escalating anxiety. But with every increasing bag my wife collected, my fear brewed into anger. It all became more daggers through my heart, and fed my inner well of resentment against her all the more.

After the rush of personalizing the rooms of the house wore off, the cold fear of stillness crept up my spine like oncoming pneumonia. Still unable to sleep, all I could do was pull my knees toward my chest and rock myself while hoping to keep my phantoms at bay.

The next day, after an early morning workout, I put in a full day at work, which included chipping away at mounds upon mounds of paperwork. I then spent hours on the phone returning calls to people who were desperate for advice and comfort regarding their past issues of abuse. Then, with my routine completed and back at home, I wasn't sure what to do.

Usually, once home from work, I'd take the dogs out for several long walks. Then, I'd plan or cook dinner for Marsha and me. Alone as a couple, we'd spend our time dissecting and hashing out our latest strings of crises. And because I was almost always recovering from the intensity of being on the road, often having traveled through several time zones, I would beg off and go to bed early, leaving my wife to her television shows while she scrutinized and dog-eared the pages of her pile of fashion magazines.

I knew my wife was unhappy. But I found myself just trying to regenerate to fight the same battles the next day. It all became a cycle. I became more distant and more shut down with each passing day, and it left me more exhausted than the day before. In the back of my mind I was still very dedicated to my marital vows, and I clung to the belief that tomorrow would be the day I'd summit my last mountain. After taking care of everything and everyone, I would *then* dedicate time to my marriage.

Home by myself with hours to spare before I could limp to bed and pray for sleep, I quickly surveyed the house. Knowing I couldn't rearrange anything else, I glanced outside and came up with an idea. A short time later I returned from the nearby nursery with my SUV completely crammed with flowers, assorted pots, and a small mountain of soil. Like a whirlwind, I raced to plant and arrange my flowers in a precise way. In less than a week, I had flowers everywhere—in ascending sizes of ceramic pots, in hanging baskets under a large umbrella, on the stairs, and stacked beside the wall of the house. Anywhere one looked, one could see my fiery creation.

I quickly discovered that I could spend two to maybe three hours of my day picking off the dead buds or simply puttering away outside. As a child in the basement, I had dreamt of being in the sun. Now it didn't matter that the temperature was into three digits, or how humid the weather or how dirty I became, I was creating something out of nothing. I was beautifying my new life. And by changing my environment, that in itself would change my life.

But it wasn't until late one night, exhausted and famished as I surveyed my work, that I felt it, that slow, receding sensation from my latest distraction. I surprised myself by finally admitting that once again, all I had done was find another escape. I did so in part so I wouldn't have to deal with, let alone *feel*, all that I had kept suppressed. Even with all the brightly colored beauty of my creation surrounding me, I felt hollow and dark within.

I felt light-headed. I noticed my right hand begin to tremble. I looked down, discovering I was turning in small circles. Becoming more faint, I wanted to scream to myself, "Not now! I don't have time for this."

From one of my deeply buried boxes within myself, I began to feel the same acute tension I had felt when I was Mother's terrified prisoner. Back then I had vowed to do my best and rely only on myself, although surviving on a daily if not hourly basis made my promise nearly impossible.

Besides the humiliation and torture, Mother loved nothing more than at the end of the day, after my laundry list of chores was completed, to shove a plate of cold leftover food in front of me. Like a dog that was trained to heel, I was not permitted to move a muscle while Mother ranted nonstop. Without her knowing, I would try to draw in any scent of the food, sometimes thinking back to the time when I was allowed to be a member of the family and eat at the end of the long, majestic, decorated table. When Mother stopped fuming, I could hear her take in a deep breath. I knew what was coming next. From behind, I could feel Mother's warm, rancid breath. "You have thirty seconds to eat your meal."

On the outside, I shivered, in part from my mother's demented pleasure. Yet on the inside I beamed, knowing full well I had earned my prize. All the while I told myself, "I can eat a lot in thirty seconds."

On one such occasion, before I could reach out and shove the soggy food into my mouth, Mother snatched the plate away and threw the contents into the garbage disposal. It all happened faster than I could blink. Dumbstruck, all I could do was turn to the right and gape upward toward Mother as she scraped every bit from the plate. My mind sped off, thinking how I had done everything to meet her impossible standards. Daring to look at her face, I wanted to state, "That's not fair, I earned it."

Then, as if sensing my shock, Mother flashed me one of her evil smiles just before she announced, "Too slow. Too bad. Maybe next time."

Alone in the basement I spent hours beating myself up replaying, then dissecting all that I might have done wrong—maybe my eyes revealed my anxiousness, maybe I breathed the wrong way, or maybe my head was not bent down as far as it should have been. After running through my cycle, all I could do was apply my focus to thinking of what I could do the next time. For the most part, my energy and effort were nothing more than a waste. I never could come up with a golden egg, a prize to appease Mother, a silver bullet to stop her once and for all.

After Mother and Father separated, all that I knew was gone. After years of endless days of prayer and coming up with outlandish plans to steal food or counter Mother's physical attacks, I was done. Inside, I was dead. I actually prayed for death.

Sometimes, late at night, Mother would summon me up from the bottom of the basement stairs. When I reached the top stair, she would wrap her hands around my neck and squeeze as if wringing out a rag. Once, with the heels of my feet dangling over the edge and feeling the pressure behind my eyes build, thinking she wouldn't stop until she'd crushed my throat, I looked Mother in the eye. My stare pierced through hers, and from within,

I screamed. From the depths of my being, I cried for her to end it. With whatever energy I somehow had stored in reserve, with my eyes, I deliberately egged her on. If she could kill me, I could finally rest in peace. And while I believed I would go to heaven, Mother would spend the rest of her life trapped in the loneliness and hatred of her own world.

Somehow, I knew that Mother was exhausted from fighting to keep our secret hidden from the many people that obviously knew the truth. She constantly had to justify to my bewildered brothers her treatment of me. And judging by her labored breathing, her puffy face, and how she dragged herself throughout the house, I knew she was completely miserable.

Once rescued and placed in foster care I discovered, to my horror, that in a few years, once I "aged out," I would be solely responsible for my own being. Fearful of ending up homeless like my father, I came up with simple, perhaps foolish plans to build up and save financial reserves. At times I became frantic, sprinting from job to job, constantly plotting where I had to go and exactly what I had to do next.

As an air crew member with the military, I altered how I used my time. I came to multitask so well that in the middle of a war, I could flawlessly orchestrate and refuel eight fighter jets in mere minutes, as if I were directing some aerial ballet. And even in life-threatening, extremely time-sensitive in-flight emergencies (IFEs), I thrived on the adrenaline. It seemed that the methods of disconnecting that I had learned in the basement now aided me in controlling my own sphere.

For years, as a civilian, when things seemed their worst and all time seemed lost, somehow I was fortunate enough to push through. Whether I missed a flight, lost luggage, or had to change into a suit and tie while driving at warp speed, I managed to spilt mere nanoseconds of time.

Since my days in the basement, I was always hypervigilant of the amount of time required to resolve any situation.

But with my wife's departure and our marital problems seemingly gone with her, I was astonished that I could no longer deny my deep-rooted issues of control, especially that of managing time.

I only ate once a day. Sometimes, in the early evening hours after a long day at work, I would go out for food. But I always took my dinner to go so I could race back to the safety of my home. Then as my "reward," I would eat my lukewarm food in my darkened bedroom in front of the droning television set.

And now, alone to admire my latest accomplishment, outside in the stillness of the evening, I could feel my insides becoming unglued. A part of me that I had buried long ago was erupting to the surface.

Every waking day I did all that I could to push down and conceal my guilt, shame, and anger. As much as I tried to open up and trust someone besides my own son, Stephen, I became more and more disconnected.

I could feel the familiar sensation of my throat tightening, the burning hiccups surging, the gasping for air. I bent over with tears of pain. As I fell to my knees, I felt it was vital for me to keep my eyes fixed on the brightly colored flowers. While my spasms increased, I could no longer keep from throwing up. With all the bile that escaped, I cried with newly released inner rage.

CHAPTER 4

THE RUINOUS PURGE

I COULD NO LONGER DENY the hard fact that my past, in more ways than I wished to count, was catching up with me. My entire life, in one way or another, had always been based on stringent safeguards. But after my latest incident, along with the weight of my divorce, the pillars of my foundation were beginning to crumble.

Days after my recurring illness, when I was working outside, I could still make out the washed outline on the gray cement. Even though it was barely visible and I felt certain that no one else would ever notice, I knew what was once there and what it represented.

Just contemplating the mere thought of losing so much in such a short period of time incensed me. But before my anger could build any further, I glanced at the dark green cascading vines and the bright orange and purple impatiens flowers. They flushed away my anxiety. For the most part, whenever I reached critical mass, at the heart of everything, I always realized that I was extremely lucky. From the moment when I first opened my eyes every morning to the end of the day, no matter how grueling or hectic, I knew how fortunate I was to simply be alive.

In foster care, I once became sick in front of the entire student body in the junior high cafeteria. After that I learned that because Mother had had me swallow ammonia twice in a twenty-four-hour period, I was lucky to be able to breathe, let alone swallow food. Later when a doctor tried to explain to me, a wide-eyed boy with a hypersonic thought process, I listened but was dismissive about my condition's possible long-term effects. As a young teenager, I didn't allow the pertinent information to seep in.

Just as I had always internally programmed myself to deal with the shame and guilt from my past, I simply covered up my problem. I adjusted. I hid in plain sight. I stayed away from particular foods. I learned to eat in certain ways—my bites were smaller, and I chewed more quickly. But once, after years of continuing to deny my problem, I was being honored with an award at an elaborate dinner ceremony and my insecurity nearly triggered another incident. Terrified and embarrassed, I floundered to maintain control. I eventually recovered with no one the wiser, but from then on I adjusted by avoiding eating in public settings. Like many times in my past, I built a labyrinth of cocoons to ensure my protective isolation.

After a few years, and with constant practice, I pushed aside my reality and even bought into my own deception. Because my incidents were rare—two, maybe three times a year—I attributed them to too much work, extensive traveling, or lack of rest. At home, when my body fought to recover, my justifications branched out to include the wrong foods, too much coffee, my love of cooking thick tomato sauce with freshly pressed garlic, and even my occasional cigar.

I didn't want to accept my past as a problem, and if it came up, I would deal with it by simply pushing through.

But that was then, seemingly a different lifetime ago. The day Marsha fled, I was on the road. That evening, not knowing of my wife's early departure, my numbed mind spun out different scenarios of the certain drama of facing Marsha before she flew off. Late into the evening, exhausted, I finally fell into a fitful sleep. It seemed the moment I could feel myself float away, I startled myself awake with violent hiccups. I didn't even have the time to flee to the bathroom. I threw up on myself and the hotel bed.

After trying to clean the sheets by washing them in the shower, I spent the remainder of the night contemplating the fact that if I had not awoken myself, I could have choked on my own vomit. But once my fear faded, my pattern of dismissal went with it. I had the gall to believe that when my wife flew off, my stress triggers would flee with her.

Now in the late afternoon, after plucking off dead flowers, I once again got down on my hands and knees and struggled to scour away any remaining traces of my bile. Later that evening, still unable to sleep, I found myself massaging my throat. Without fail, even decades after the incident, I connected to the immense sickness of my perpetrator.

The first time Mother had me swallow the ammonia, I had no idea of its possible effects. Even as she made a dramatic demonstration of preparing my latest form of punishment, I truly had very little concern over its outcome. Since it was late at night, and I had been refused food, I was tired and too worn out to analyze the magnitude of my situation.

The very next afternoon, Mother showed off to Father with a repeat performance. As I backed into my father's detached frame as a form of protection, I was fighting to keep my mouth shut to avoid a single drop. I didn't raise my hand. I didn't run off. I never stood up for myself, not even by proclaiming the simplest of commands: "No. Stop." In other words, I swallowed whatever my perpetrator dished out.

After ingesting the cleaner, like the night prior, the inside of my throat suddenly felt as if it were on fire. At the same time, my trachea closed off. Unable to draw in a single molecule of air, I collapsed directly in front of my father's feet. I used both of my tiny red fists to pound the multicolored spotted floor with the desperate hope this somehow would permit me to breathe.

But it didn't. With every wretched second, I felt myself slipping away. Then in pure, molten rage, with all the strength I had left, I looked up at my father's statue-like body. From the deepest part of my being, I screeched at Mother, Father, and then, myself. The very next second Mother bent down to slap me on my upper back, which finally permitted to me to breathe.

Still on my knees, I gulped in as much air as possible. With my strained vision beginning to clear, I glanced up at both parents. I had known and accepted just how sinister and sick Mother was the day she burned my arm on the gas stove. And with every escalating situation, I saw and felt how broken and disconnected my father had become. Out of the three of us in that closed setting, I felt I was the only person who was actually sane. I wasn't mentally ill, or detached, in part, from alcohol. I had a razor-sharp mind and the hidden power of raw determination.

But I lacked the courage to prevent the obvious.

As an adult, in the solitude of my private setting, the price I still pay for my inaction as a child is not only the swirl of frustrating emotions, but the increasing anxiety of being too afraid to simply breathe.

CHAPTER 5

THE BLACK HOLE

FOR THE LIFE OF ME, I COULD NOT SLEEP. No matter the intensity of my actions throughout the day, at work or at home, rest was somehow beyond my reach. And with each passing day, I only felt more drained, my thoughts stuck in a murky soup of fog.

When I was on the road, in hotels or even in airports, with an hour or two of rest, I did fine. My adrenaline pulled me through. But for some unknown reason, in my beautiful home, I could rarely capture more than a single hour of sleep.

And, no matter what tactic I attempted, my results always ended in failure.

It wasn't always like that. As a child, sleep had been my purest form of escape. In the bottom of the basement, days after Mother had stabbed me in the chest and refused to take me to the hospital, the gash became infected. After squeezing out the pus from my wound, I half limped, half crawled over to the base of the stairs. Proud and exhausted from my accomplishment, I rewarded myself by completely shutting down with sleep. I was fully aware that if Mother suddenly opened the door to check on me, she would have another excuse to brutalize me. I didn't give a damn. Later that afternoon, I escaped the misery of my world by visualizing I wore a cape of red and flew at fantastic speeds high among the clouds.

Even when Mother had me sit on top of my hands in the rocky section of the fog-filled backyard, I was somehow able to daydream about the better times of my past, of family vacations to the Russian River, and the one special time Mother selected me to fish with her. I was able to find that internal switch that enabled me to find my reprieve.

As an adult, sometimes on the road I would literally be behind a stage, where I'd use my battered brown satchel as a pillow and lie on my back, close my eyes, and slow my breathing until I could feel myself drift away.

But now I had lost one of my most vital protective mechanisms. And when I did sleep, I was haunted by nightmares of my perpetrator.

During my time in foster care, whenever I had nightmares of Mother she would be chasing me through a narrow, endless maze, wielding the same knife as she had when she had stabbed me in the chest. I could never run fast enough or far enough to escape the blade from plunging into me. Yet, the thing that frightened me the most were Mother's red, hate-filled eyes. Then, for some reason, after my father passed away, when Mother pursued me in my dreams I suddenly stopped running, stood my ground, and my phantom vanished.

But now when I dreamt of Mother she seemed like an inescapable specter of death. After Marsha and I separated, in the first series of dreams of Mother, I was locked to a chair in some darkened, medieval dungeon.

In one dream, after sensing a putrid odor, I could make out Mother at the far end of a long rectangular table, with her gnarled, clenched fingers from years of painful arthritis and a gray-white mop covering her face. She was dressed in a black smock-like dress. For some reason, she seemed to hover just above the floor. When her tangled strands of hair parted, it revealed a thick, swollen face with sunken, dark, unmoving eyes.

As Mother slowly studied me, I could feel the temperature of the room become frigid. Then, without moving her lips, inside my head she stated, "After all you've accomplished, you have been and always will be absolutely nothing." I knew that she wanted me to feel the dagger-like force of every syllable. A stream of coughs interrupted her sledgehammer of words. "Understand, you are now and always will be nothing to anyone or to anything. You are nothing... without me."

She stopped to let another cough from deep within escape her failing lungs. Then in a slower, more deliberate cadence, Mother continued, "If they only knew you like I do. If anyone were ever to find out the *real* David Pelzer, what do you think would happen?" Again, there came a long, chilling pause. "I know you." She emphasized these words by pointing a crooked finger at me. "Why do you think *you* sabotage anything and everyone that ever gets near you?

"Maybe they don't see it? Maybe you've got them all conned? But I see right through you. I always have. I always will," she scoffed.

I felt as if I had been confined for years and I was feeling whatever strength I had slip away.

Inside my head, in perfect clarity, Mother continued, "You were always weak. You never had any backbone. Why do you think I chose you? You're so pathetic. You could have stopped it all then. Just like you could stop it all right now. The truth is you can't, because *you* won't. You lived for it then and you'll live for it now. You live for me."

I blinked, refocusing my eyes to just above hers. With the tiniest of movements, I saw Mother's lips move while her words simultaneously ricocheted inside my head. Looking directly into her morbid eyes, I surprised myself by asking, "What do you want?"

Tilting her head as if I were some alien from another planet that she wished to study, she fired back, "No, no, no. Wrong question." She nodded as if I was supposed to understand another one of her twisted, cryptic games.

As if she were ready to reveal a wide smile, Mother seemed so pleased with herself. "The question is not what I want." After a slight gasp, she continued, "What is it that *you* so desperately seek?" She then paused as if for her own amusement. "Why am I here? What is it that you want… from me?"

I fought to clear my head. Even though I felt it was too late, I didn't want to take the chance of allowing Mother to dig too deeply inside me.

Her hacking cough brought my attention back to the far end of the table. I could hear the distinctive rhythmic clicking of her long, blackened fingernails on the wood. "So, now that she's gone, the second one, and now that you have everything all to yourself, why would you bring me back? What is it about me that you can't… live… without?"

Without any feelings of weakness, resentment, pain, or even the slightest hint of revenge, I was stymied. It was as if someone had suddenly thrown cold water on me. I shook my head clear. In the rarest of moments, I didn't overly analyze or hide behind a facade. I replied with the first thought that came from both my brain and my heart. "I honestly don't know."

Leaning forward, as if willing to reveal the absolute secret of the universe, Mother whispered, "I do."

Her last words hung in the air like bubbles just before the increasing pressure made them pop. Inside my mind, I fought to snap out of my trance. I felt the sensation of my heart racing as well as a thick, sticky layer of sweat covering my skin. My sole focus was to keep Mother from penetrating my tiny mental lockbox. If she broke in, I felt I would be completely helpless and forever stuck in this hell with her.

I remained passive, hoping I didn't reveal any fear. But her proclamation hit too close to the bone. I fought to think of something else. A familiar smell from my past filled my head—the slight musty scent from the basement where I spent so much time as Mother's prisoner.

The pressure inside my head increased. I felt as if the veins in my forehead were going to burst through at any moment. I told myself I could not allow Mother to come any closer. Ever so slowly, I heard in precise cadence, "David, it's you who can't let me go."

Suddenly, the table disappeared and Mother was mere inches in front of me. I clamped my eyes shut, but I could still see her. She was so close I could feel the coldness that encased her entire being. I tried to twist away, to escape to somewhere else, but I couldn't. The temperature dropped further, and an invisible finger lifted my chin. Smiling for her own enjoyment, Mother then announced, "I know what you desire. I know what you crave." Leaning closer, she shook her head. "Not now. Not ever. I will never allow it. I will never grant you peace."

Shaking my head to clear it from my nightmare, I became incensed that in my weakness, I had allowed my perpetrator to again have so much control over me. As much as I craved sleep, part of me now feared what lay in wait on the other side.

CHAPTER 6

A THOUSAND NEEDLES

WITH EVERY PASSING DAY I felt I was losing my footing. No matter what I did, no matter what direction I tried to turn, I either set off a minefield from my buried past or I stupidly wandered into a pit of psychological quicksand.

The pressures that increased with each new day became too much. I could rarely sleep, and when I did I had nightmares that made me snap awake, covered in sweat. Because of my throat, I became too afraid to eat and began to forgo food even more. Once a day when I grabbed something to eat, I'd rush back home to nibble my prize, just in case my throat "acted up."

I couldn't swallow anymore. I was feeling despair, rejection, guilt, shame, and the constant dread of being so afraid. It was killing me. And it seemed that whenever I was able to capture a moment of stillness, a moment to clear my mind and push aside my issues, allow myself to relax, something would always come up. Feeling vulnerable and craving the sensation of wanting to be wanted, I'd immediately allow outside situations to take over my solace.

The latest matter was with my former wife Marsha. It started one afternoon when I was on the road, during a free moment, when without thinking I lowered my guard and phoned her. After exchanging salutations and her telling me about her endless adventures in shopping that included securing a Cadillac sofa with fin tails and blinking lights, Marsha announced that she hadn't felt this happy in years. My insides began to spool up.

"Dave," Marsha began, "I'm not trying to run you down, but I no longer have to dread crawling out of bed worrying what's going to fall from the sky today. As your director, every day I'm on the phone—you have no idea! I'd get the sickos—screaming at me, vomiting all their disgusting filth and how they demand that you instantly drop whatever you're doing, fly out to wherever, and live with them and save them from all their issues. Can you imagine how hard this is for me?" Her voice cracked through the strain.

"I couldn't do it anymore, Dave. Fighting to justify to those crazy, blood-sucking idiots you needing just two hours of sleep a night."

Rolling on, Marsha continued, "Then when you came home you were more like some handyman taking care of the house and then, whoosh, you were gone. And when you had more than two days off in a row, it never failed, you would collapse. You wouldn't let me near you, and you certainly wouldn't go to the doctor."

She paused as if to collect her thoughts. "I thought things would slow down, but they didn't, and it only got weirder. I tried. But I couldn't do it anymore. I just got tired of you flying off to rescue others and not being there for me. It's not the life for me and it's not my idea of a marriage."

Suddenly my blood began to race. My mind flipped a switch. I thought, "Hey, *I'm* the one out there working my tail off, driving at all hours, going without food and sleep for days. I'm not out power shopping or taking all those vacations every few weeks! *You're* not being fair." I screamed to myself, wanting to lash back at Marsha to *make* her, force her, to understand. "You ran the office; you knew, planned, and approved everything in my life!"

But as much as my ego got in the way, I knew she was right. Everything about me was beyond excessive. "Marsha, I am sorry. So sorry. I… I tried, I really did." I shook my head from side to side, trying to justify all my former actions. Above all, more than anything, I wanted to prove to Marsha…

But before I could swim after Marsha's approval, she dropped the bomb. "Dave, I met someone."

All I could do was stare at the phone. The more Marsha gently tried to explain her situation, the more I could feel myself becoming lost in an endless maze of fog. Finally, I coughed up a quick good-bye and, wanting Marsha to feel just an ounce of my pain, I snapped the phone shut before she could state anything else.

I struggled to concentrate on breathing. My hand was coiled around the cellphone as if it were a boa constrictor. My grip was so tight I thought I'd snap the device in two. I slowly sat back up when I felt the oxygen return to my head.

I felt like some dormant volcano. With every ounce of my being, I wanted to stand up and spew the lava of despair that I had kept buried below the surface for so long.

When I finally calmed down, I knew I had nothing to be jealous about. Because of her erratic, emotional-roller-coaster behavior, as well as her shopping binges, I had known for years that Marsha was extremely unhappy and burnt out. As mad as I was at Marsha, at the end of the day, I only had myself to blame. Because I felt betrayed and that my trust was constantly violated, whenever the newest batches of Marsha's bills came past due, it was me who called it quits.

A sense of abandonment took over. It didn't help when I received letters from Marsha that included reams of pictures showing off her new, custom-made house, the cars that she somehow purchased every few months, the dogs dressed in various attire, and her elaborate trip to the Super Bowl. But when I saw photos of Marsha standing next to her immaculately groomed new beau, I nearly vomited in my mouth.

I should have simply ripped them up. But I didn't. Instead, I'd spend hours dissecting the smallest nuance of every picture. Even though I fumed with each photograph, I never stopped my obsessive examinations. I knew I didn't have to look at my former wife's new life. And that I shouldn't even open the damned envelopes.

But my longing to feel wanted overruled sensible logic, which overruled my pain. At least, I told myself, I was worthy enough that Marsha, with her high-end new life, still even thought of me.

In part because of my low self-esteem, my constant quest for approval, even the sickening thread of Marsha's correspondence helped to pull me through.

I also gained the satisfaction that I had not totally contaminated someone close to me with my past and the issues that I carried with it. And if only for a moment, *that* in itself gave me a sense of peace.

CHAPTER 7

LEFT BEHIND

FOR THE LONGEST TIME, while taking insomnia-inspired late-night walks, I brooded about my former life with my wife. As much as my ego did not want to accept it, to be brutally honest, part of me was resentful that in less than two months from our separation, Marsha was with someone else. And seeing her photos of her continuous outings with descriptive captions was like jamming the ice pick deeper into my side.

My feelings were self-centered and completely childish. With each step I took in the cool night air among the desert palm trees, I detested myself for my junior high—like sentiment and weakness.

I used to be stronger. I used to have an impregnable barrier of defense, a stronger flip switch that I had developed back in the days as Mother's prisoner. I had honed my skill so well that even when she was a mere inch from my face, spewing her toxic hatred against me and her rain of saliva splattering my face, her words had no meaning to me. I was so deeply disconnected it was like a thick wall of water between us.

In foster care, and later in strenuous courses with the military, whenever I was bullied or hard-pressed, I remained passive on the outside and didn't allow anything to penetrate. Once, after a burly instructor ripped into me, I was asked about my detached behavior by one of my peers, who too was yelled at and seemed on the verge of losing it. I joked, "Yeah, the sarge's a badass, but he ain't got *nothing* when it comes to my mom."

Even separating with Stephen's mother, Patsy, as painful as it was, especially being away from my beloved son, hadn't stung this much.

As I walked one evening, I lingered outside, stopping when I came to the crest of a small hill. I stared down at the fog that had completely enveloped the cove in which I resided. The swirling gray thickness reminded me of the Bay Area and how quickly the mist made everything disappear. In my increasingly stewing, sleep-deprived state, I thought of a time when I felt devalued and invisible in plain sight.

It was an Indian summer in the Bay Area and everything was crisp, bright, beautiful, and warm. Even when I was forced to run from school to Mother's house, I soaked in the outside world like a gigantic sponge. I cheated by slowing my pace to capture every sight, smell, sound, and most importantly for me, the sun's embracing rays. It was enough to get by. And it was so much more than I'd had before.

After doing my midafternoon chores, rather than sitting at the bottom of the basement stairs, Mother had me sit in the corner of the garage beside Father's long-neglected workbench. I quickly discovered the hardness of the cement floor made my muscles ache far more than sitting on top of my hands on the wooden stairs.

As was always the case with Mother, there was a method to her madness. Moving me to the corner was not just another perverted form of torture, but a convenience for her and The Family. As her boys ran up and down the stairs, I would have been in their way—physically and psychologically.

With my head bowed down, a gurgling stomach, and numbed hands, I was almost past my limit. My mind began to swim with colliding currents of immense self-pity, frustration with myself for allowing this to go on as long as it had, and the building disdain I held against Father and recently even against my own brothers.

Before my baby brother, Kevin, was born, I discovered that my avenue of escape, shutting down and dreaming myself away, was becoming less and less effective for me. Back before kindergarten, sleep was my secret refuge. When I was literally starving, I'd dream about thick, juicy hamburgers smothered with every conceivable condiment, oozing with bright, bubbling orange cheese.

But I eventually became too jaded and disillusioned to even fantasize. Resentment began to take root, first toward myself, but then quickly also toward those around me. I knew it was wrong, completely wrong, to have feelings of hatred. But deep down inside I cried and screamed at myself for allowing the situation to intensify, and the sensation fed me. It kept me warm. It provided me with a sense of control. It helped dilute some of the shame and loneliness that never seemed to escape me.

Just a few feet away, The Family celebrated the unseasonably warm weather with a barbecue. The high-pitched screeches and nonstop laughter echoed throughout the garage. It seemed as if every kid was enjoying themselves in the day's splendor. From the distinctive scent of charcoal and sizzling food, it also seemed that every family on the entire Norman Rockwell-like, goody-goody, small-town-USA block was making the most of the rare occasion.

My breathing increased as my heart began to race. I swelled with jealousy. Nearby, Ron bounced back and forth, up and down the stairs, happily carrying supplies for the cookout.

Father had allowed Ron to cook the burgers and hot dogs. Since Ron was the oldest, it was a huge privilege. With every trip back down the stairs before he dashed outside, he yelled out the updates: "Everyone showed up"; "Man, is it hot!"; "You should see it, it's a blast!" The digs seemed to get a little bit more personal. "Man, there is sooooo much food. Everyone brought over everything. I just hope it doesn't all go to waste. Now, that would be a real shame."

At that moment, I detested him.

Ron knew I was hungry, that I heard, felt, and practically drooled over every word. He knew that I shivered as he passed by. Ron, who used to sneak me food, knew that I was real and that I did exist.

While I was sure his statements were playful, Ron's words hit me like a sledgehammer.

In a flash, I slipped. I lost control and abandoned all self-imposed discipline. I stepped outside of my protective shield, broke all the rules. My rules.

With sarcastic punch, I boldly stated, "Thanks for the burger… man!"

Ron stopped in midstride. If it weren't for his right hand that gripped the staircase railing, he would have toppled head over. His eyes gleamed. I then picked up on his expression, which seemed to say, "I'm gonna tell Mom and you're so gonna get it."

I returned, without a spoken word, "Like… I… really… care."

In reality, the incident lasted a mere second. Yet by lashing out, especially to someone I truly cared about, it somehow transferred the weight of my pain away from me, if only for a moment. I fully understood my situation was not in any way Ron's fault, but over the years, it had become painfully obvious to both of us that we were from two different worlds.

Soon after Ron ambled back outside, I overheard the inevitable question arise. For the past few years, whenever a group of neighbors gathered, somebody would inquire: "Cathy, where is that boy of yours… David? I only catch a glimpse of him whenever he's running to or from school."

Mother would always try to laugh it off. The first time I heard the question, Mother's hesitation belied her dismay. Someone had actually said something. Yet over time the response simply became, "Oh, the boy's just sick. Touch of the flu. Caught a bad cold."

That time, from the corner of the garage, as scores of individuals enjoyed the early autumn day, I heard it. The slight yet hesitant follow-up, "But Cathy, wouldn't the warm sunshine do David some good?"

The world seemed to stop. The sound of silence suddenly enveloped the party. I could imagine Mother avoiding any eye contact, hoping to scurry away and do something, anything, other than stand in front of other adults and be held accountable.

"Um, well, Cathy," the guest continued, "what do you think?"

"Well, it's like I said, the boy's sick. Too sick. You wouldn't want him to pass it along. I'm sure it's probably contagious. Now, if you'll excuse me, I do have to go check on… something."

After a few seconds, I could hear the same lady speaking to someone else: "Who does she think she's kidding? I asked her that same thing the last time. If it's true, that little boy is the sickest child on this planet."

A new voice chimed in, "Let me tell you, the last time I saw David, he looked like a ghost. Pasty, pale white skin, sunken eyes. I tell you, it was just horrible… can you imagine even having to *look* at that?"

"And did you catch how Cathy doesn't even call him by name? That's just horrible, just horrible. There's something definitely wrong," the first lady relayed. But a heartbeat later the same voice transformed from concern to excitement. "The burgers are ready! Let's go get us something to eat. I'm famished."

Part of me was ecstatic that I was even thought of, that after all those years someone had actually noticed my absence, that someone had stood up to Mother, even if just for a moment.

But in the end, as usual, it didn't amount to anything.

With the distinctive smells and clattering sounds from outside filling the garage, I became disgusted with *myself.* For God's sake, all I had to do was stand up and walk out for all to see. Then, I could reach out, seize something to eat, and sprint off into the sunset. In less than a minute, my life would change. I knew that if I even dared, everyone—the neighbors, my brothers, Father, and especially the former Cub Scouts den mother extraordinaire, Mrs. Pelzer—would be frozen in complete shock.

But I did nothing. I simply stayed out of sight and, to others around me, out of mind.

Besides my father, the one adult who knew what was happening under my parents' roof, but who too decided to turn a blind eye, was my mother's mother.

Later, as an adult, I came to realize the common thread between mother and daughter.

In the rare family photos taken with Grandmother, she was always as stiff as a board. She never seemed to even attempt to crack a smile, let alone have physical contact with anyone. I could not recall Grandmother ever giving anybody a warm embrace, letting out a laugh, or paying someone a sincere compliment. The inflection of her every word was condescending. And, I came to believe, she enjoyed it.

It never seemed to matter to Grandmother what others were doing or how they went about living their lives, because when Grandmother arrived, it was suddenly and completely *her* world. And God forbid anyone hesitated to instantly conform to her ways.

As a very young child, I had heard how Grandmother, a widow, had raised Mother and my uncle Dan alone in the middle of the Depression. And I truly admired that. As fierce and independent as Grandmother was, she was also the smartest person I knew. As a child, I would have given anything to sit down in a chair with my feet dangling just above the floor and take in all that Grandmother had experienced: stories about listening to old radio shows or relaying the sensation of her first flight aboard a sleek jet aircraft. It was all so fascinating to me.

But that was just another stupid childish fantasy that I had to switch off.

Before things became too bizarre between Mother and me, whenever Grandmother showed up, usually unannounced, Mother would literally lock up. Her body would become tense and her voice became either meek or sarcastic. As preschoolers, Ron, Stan, and I were instructed to play "extra, extra quiet" in our room or outside so as not to upset Grandmother; to be seen for a moment or two, but definitely never heard.

Because we'd play so quietly, the three of us could hear the eventual volley from the kitchen:

"Mother, please," Mother would beg.

Grandmother would huff, "I don't understand. If it was up to me, I certainly would have done it different. Let me tell you something, back in my day, I wouldn't put up with any of this. Not one damn bit. Not for one day. And I'll tell you something else—"

"Mother, please," our mother would fight to insert, "the children are going to hear you. Please!"

"Jesus H. Christ, Roerva, I'm not saying one damn thing. Not one damn thing..."

The room would become quiet, then after a slight pause Grandmother would resume, "For God's sake, all I'm saying is you could have done better. I'm not telling you how to live your life, I'm not telling you what to do, but—"

I could imagine Mother's face tensing as tight as a drum. "*That's all you do!* All the time, every hour, of every day. That's all you ever do. To Dan, his wife, his kids, my life, my husband, my kids... you've got your nose buried so far in everyone's life telling them how to live, it's a wonder you can barely breathe!

"Does anyone ever tell you anything, ever? You put everyone through absolute hell and you love it."

"Well, in all my life... I never..." Grandmother would say. "Let me tell you something, Roerva Catherine Pelzer, back in my day, you never, never talked back, let alone raise your voice to your elders. I'm so ashamed for you. All I wanted, all I've ever wanted was..." Grandmother would trail off as if the pain she endured was just too much to go on.

"Enough!" Mother would state, standing her ground.

"Well, I certainly didn't raise you to be disrespectful to your parents."

"Parents?" Mother lobbed back.

"Your father... well, that man is another story. To hell with him. To hell with you and everyone else. I did my best. I did all that I could. But it was never enough. Never enough for the likes of you. Never.

"And another thing, you watch your tone with me. I'm still your mother. Hell's bells, back in the day I remember whenever you got too big for your britches, that's when a good bar of soap crammed down that throat of yours and a good sound thrashing would put you in your place. That's how you got things done, let me tell you."

After every argument, Grandmother would depart, but not before issuing a stern warning for the three of us preschoolers to be good.

Starting when I was in the first grade, more than once Grandmother marched into our bedroom to find me staring straight into the mirror stating, "I'm a bad boy. I'm a bad boy," for hours as punishment for my latest misdeeds. The first time she saw me in front of the reflective glass, I was surprised by her sudden presence and almost accidentally stopped. But out of fear of Mother, I quickly recovered. Hovering above me, with her boney hands on her slender hips, Grandmother shook her head. "For Christ's sake, if you're not the sorriest child I have ever known." She continued to stare down at me without a word, without a touch to my shoulder, before turning away and stomping down the hallway.

In later years, when I lived in the basement, contact with Grandmother was reduced to her opening the door to the basement for a second or two. In February of 1973, after my parents separated, Grandmother made a surprise visit. In typical fashion, she began, "What did I tell you? Did I not tell you this would happen? Did I? Well?"

I listened, knowing that after Grandmother stormed off, hell would follow. Yet they couldn't get enough of each other. If it wasn't the face-to-face battle royales, they'd blast each other several times a day on the phone for hours at a time. I came to conclude that they fed off each other's complete and absolute misery.

That February, just a few weeks before my sudden rescue, during her last visit, the last words I heard from Grandmother came when she flung open the basement door and flipped on the light switch to examine me where I sat at the base of the steps, on top of my hands, with my soiled face tilted upward. She declared, "Hell's bells, if that isn't cold."

That day, for a mere second, I was almost certain that our eyes locked. But not being allowed to wear my glasses unless at school, I couldn't be sure. Deep down, for a split second, I had so craved not only that my relative saw me, but that in some small way, I mattered.

Somewhere beneath the layers of hardened control and anger, I sensed a thread that Grandmother cared. I was forever grateful to Grandmother because she was in fact the person who had initiated my removal by personally calling social services on my mother a full year before I was rescued.

Yet, Grandmother visited me only once at my first permanent foster home in South San Francisco. During the visit, I overheard her declare to my foster mother, Mrs. Cantanze, "I see no need to cry over spilled milk. It's really no one's damn business. Opening up Pandora's box never did anyone any good. What happens in the house should stay in the house."

My protective foster parent jumped in. "Excuse me, but you're not making any sense."

Mrs. Cantanze didn't know it, but she had just done the unthinkable: 1) she interrupted Grandma, and 2) she had the audacity to question her!

After a short moment of silence, Grandma seemed to switch tactics. "Well, I'm not saying it happened and I'm not saying it didn't..."

"Then what *are* you saying?" my foster mother dared probe.

"Well, back in my day, we never..." Grandmother prattled on as if her age-old wisdom should be instantly accepted without dispute.

Later, as Grandmother backed away in her boat-sized green four-door Oldsmobile, even though I happily waved good-bye to her, she seemed to stare through me as if I were, once again, invisible.

Standing beside me, Mrs. Cantanze stated, "The both of them, evil. Absolute evil."

Many years later, when Grandmother drove out to visit my then-infant son, she badgered me relentlessly over dinner about not returning home at *her* allocated time. It didn't matter that flying for the air force was not a nine-to-five job, or that on that day my crew and I had survived a lengthy in-flight emergency that required an extended debriefing. Grandmother's only concern seemed to be voicing her displeasure.

When Stephen's mother, Patsy, tried to deflect Grandmother by mentioning my volunteer work with troubled youth, as well as my working at the local juvenile detention center, before she could complete her sentence,

Grandmother bellowed, "If you ask me, charity starts in the home. And, if you ask me, most of them are spoiled rotten. I tell you what, if anything..."

Tired of replaying my past in the dead of the night, I realized now, as I had as a small child, that as much as Grandmother *declared* everything, she really said nothing.

That same sensation made me think of my father, who when on the job was fearless in risking his life as a firefighter, but once his uniform was removed and he had returned home, he seemed so broken that he could only feed me empty words.

Father's abandonment of me was a different story. In the beginning he was easily swayed (as was I) that I was always getting into mischief. But when he saw me go from sleeping in a bed to sleeping under the kitchen table by the kitty litter with newspapers for a blanket, and later on a cot in the basement, surely alarm bells must have gone off. And yet, nothing changed.

It was always hard to gauge Father's true feelings. As my situation became more desperate, I wanted to believe that he would insert himself if only he *could*. I also knew how much he dreaded returning home from a twenty-four-hour shift at the station only to face Mother's bizarre behavior.

One afternoon, to my surprise, I returned from school to find Father and I had the house to ourselves. As if *he* were nervous from doing something he was not supposed to, Father presented me with a thick Swiss cheese sandwich oozing with dark mustard and mayonnaise. I didn't understand—my father had made something for me? As he curtly instructed me, I devoured my prize as fast as possible. As I gulped down a glass of milk, I could see Father nervously spying the kitchen clock just above his shoulders.

Then without any compassion he barked, "You better get to work on your chores. And for God's sakes, keep your mouth shut. Don't you tell her a damn thing. I can't help you if she finds out."

Like a dog that just got swatted on the nose, I lowered my head and gave a slight nod that I understood. But for a rare moment, Father loved me so much that he made me a sandwich.

Every once in a while when I was washing the dinner dishes, Father would try to help by putting a few away in the cupboards that were too tall for me to reach. I used to try to lean in close enough to capture a whiff of his distinctive Old Spice cologne. Since I had been trained not to look at any member of the family, I was shocked when I once stole a quick glance and saw how old and dejected he looked. His arms and face were reddened and had a thick, leathery appearance. His eyes were sunken; but what made me want to cry was how completely vacant they looked. As if Father himself was just marking time, as if he had given up.

Eventually, the only contact we had was when Father would come home from work for a few minutes to gather enough things to last him a couple of days and then flee as soon as possible. For the most part, I knew he made an effort to see me. Usually I was performing some chore for Mother when he'd bend down and whisper, "One of these days, I'm going to get you out of here. You'll see. One of these days, I'll be back for you, Tiger."

The first time he gave this promise my heart seemed to burst. Not only had he actually acknowledged the situation and was finally going to do something about it, but he had addressed me by my old childhood nickname, "Tiger," instead of as "the boy."

Father's pledge was something to cling to; it became my psychological lifeline. But the long days turned into weeks, which dragged into the change of seasons, and nothing changed. It got to the point that Father's words had no meaning to him or to me.

The last time I remember him giving me a thread of hope was while we were alone one afternoon and he suddenly grabbed my arm and spun me around. "Christ Almighty, you smell to high heaven. For God's sakes, can't you just get in the tub and—" He stopped himself midsentence.

I could feel my chest shudder. I was so ashamed of myself. I had been so obsessed with trying to meet every one of Mother's demands, as well as my own selfish quest for any scrap of food, that I never gave a single thought to how repulsive I appeared, let alone my odor.

As Father grabbed a nearby washcloth and did his best to rub the layers of grime from my face and from behind my ears, I imagined how much sensitivity he might have had for a kid he'd just snatched out from a burning building.

As if to apologize, Father muttered, "Just give me some time, a little more time. You'll see, don't you worry. I'm going to make sure I talk to her. Don't you worry, Tiger."

How I wanted to explode and shout, "One of these days! Wow! Thank you for almost thinking of me. I'm sorry I smell, but, hey, wake up, it's not like she lets me bathe, let alone wear clean clothes. Are you awake to what's happenin'? 'One of these days?' What are you gonna say, 'Gee, Roerva maybe you shouldn't, gosh, burn "the boy," maybe you shouldn't choke him until his eyes almost pop out from his head, or maybe you shouldn't throw him down the stairs! Gee!'

"I'm here. Right here, right now. Wake up, I'm your son!"

From the deepest part of my heart, I had always known that my "mommy" was sick. That there was something that made her the way she was. But I still couldn't figure out Father. In all the endless hours I spent alone shivering in the dark basement, fighting to understand my world, all I could surmise was that Father was simply broken.

The day my parents separated, I wanted to die. Mother seemed delighted to humiliate Father by presenting him with his belongings in a cardboard box in front of his cheap motel. Before Mother sped away, leaving Father in the chilling rain, she allowed him (after he asked her for permission) to come over to the car and say a few words specifically to me.

He nervously cleared his throat, then seemed to freeze up. After a few seconds of dead air, he instructed me to be good and try, "just try… ah… you know… stay out of her way." I nodded my head, trying to take in one last scent of his fragrance.

As if to say something to ease my fear, by reflex he ended with, "One of these days, Tiger… I'm gonna…"

I didn't have the strength to reassure him with a false smile. I just wanted shrink myself and hide inside his shirt pocket.

I fumed, because Father hadn't reached down and pushed that button to open the car door and simply take me away.

But, as weak as I thought Father was, so was I! *I* could have done something. *I* could have opened the passenger door back by the motel. I imagined bursting from the car and fleeing down the street, using the sheets of rain as cover, before turning into some seedy, darkened back alley. I'd hide in a wooden crate until the coast was clear. I could have lived among the homeless. Anything was better than surviving in the basement.

Even as I sulked to myself, to be perfectly honest, I barely had enough backbone to conjure a fantasy. All in all, *I* was pathetic.

And, I admitted, thirty-plus years later, I still was. As I stood staring down at the cove, I noticed my right hand beginning to tremble. Not wanting to deal with yet another problem in front of me, I dismissed the tremor.

Still wallowing in my own well of minutiae, I thought of how by protecting my own skin I had somehow turned my back on others. Immediately I thought of my brothers.

The afternoon after my rescue, when I was made a ward of the court, was bittersweet. I was free of Mother, but it came at a price. After the hearing, my social worker, Ms. Gold, walked me to her brown Chevette, and I was in the perfect position to see Mother and my brothers heading to their car. For a split second, I thought I caught a glance from Ron and Stan—a secret message that only they could give me. In less than a blink of an eye, it was gone. But their hunched shoulders made their silence scream.

With my hand wrapped around my savior's slender, gentle fingers, it hit me. I was free. But *they* still had to live with Mother. I looked up to Ms. Gold as if to ask about my brothers' safety, but the words didn't come.

As Mother's ancient silver station wagon chugged away, I concentrated on my brothers, as if to give them a protective prayer and let them know how sorry I was about everything—the lies, the sadness, the constant, immeasurable pain.

Even after the Chevy disappeared from view, I could still hear its distinctive echo. As if I had received a punch to my chest, I fought to breathe. By being saved, I had left my brothers to endure Mother's rage and demons. Now *they* were "It." By solely protecting my own hide, I had in fact left behind my own family, whom I still longed for and loved. I had abandoned *them*.

As a middle-age adult standing alone on the hill, as much as I hated to admit it, for all my righteousness and my supposed grandiose deeds, I had done more than my fair share of desertion.

CHAPTER 8

THE MAD DASH

I WAS WAY BEYOND THE POINT of being fed up. I was incensed that I couldn't get a handle on things. With every passing day, more aspects of my life seemed to fail me.

Part of my seething frustration was that as an educated adult with a plethora of over-the-top experiences behind me, I felt I was less successful than when I was merely fighting to survive. Back when I was a kid, with few to no assets, no matter how insurmountable the situation, somehow, I always found a way to pull through.

Back in Mother's basement, as I came to accept my situation I felt that I had *something*—an invisible shield of protection. Then as I grew older and experienced firsthand how others could be swallowed by seemingly insignificant events, that's when I knew for sure that *I* had my very own force field. For well over thirty years, my armored gift had rarely failed and had even helped catapult me to unimaginable heights.

But after a continual series of nightmares, I was stripped.

I knew it was entirely my fault. Through my deep-rooted anxiety, determined ego, and escalating weakness, I had lost focus, become feeble and let down my guard. And I had allowed my demon-like dream mother to invade my most cherished dream of making a connection with my deceased father.

No matter how chaotic my life was, the ability to flush everything away and escape through my dreams was my lifeline. But, after months of little rest and now with Mother infiltrating the most sacred part of my survival, I knew I was running out of steam.

I saw no solution to my inner dilemmas. With every passing day, I felt as if my life were slowly slipping from my grasp.

After initially fighting it, the recent loss of my marriage forced me to try to decipher how my past affected the many components of my life. I foolishly told myself that after I took a good, hard look at myself, I could instantly make positive steps. But I saw no light in the heart of my darkness. By recognizing some of my issues, I only felt more devastated than before. It made me want to crawl out of my own skin.

I wanted to flee from everything and everyone—particularly myself.

At times, especially at night, when I was alone and everything was still, I felt I could no longer hold it together.

Even in public, I could no longer hide. Besides my throat contractions, I had an issue with my right hand. Years ago it had been only a slight twitch at the tips of my fingers. But over time I had to clutch my left hand over my right to stop it from shaking. If I thought somebody noticed, in order not to look like a *total* idiot, I'd act as if I were playing "air piano."

As I sat outside staring at my right hand, fighting to relax by taking in the majestic beauty of the late day, I felt repulsed. My mind began to race from my pent-up anxiety. I truly felt that I had wasted too much time and energy. I began to entertain the thought of simply walking away from it all.

By instantly deflecting, I could feel my inner tension begin to subside. Running down my mental checklist, I decided all I needed was my turtle, Chuck, who had been with me since August of 1984, and a few clothes. As I felt a sense of relief, I began to smile to myself. Building momentum of feeling better, I added photos of Stephen, my twenty-year collection of books, and some office things, my CDs, DVDs, a few pieces of art. And other than that, I convinced myself I could escape my life.

I'd shut down the office and make sure that my staff, Gabbi and Rey, were properly taken care of. And with Stephen in college, and not being close to anyone, there was really very little keeping me in the Coachella Valley. "I could," I mused, "sell the house turnkey, jump in my SUV, and drive off into the sunset!"

Replaying all I had lost and missed out on, and because I had put off so much in my personal life, I actually began to believe that my plan was doable.

I took inventory. As for my *mission*, I groused, it had been hit-and-miss. I fully understood I was an odd duck. Because of my intense nervousness and my burned tongue from the times Mother had me ingest ammonia, I spoke way too fast. Since every audience was different, and I addressed as many as seven a day, I had to switch gears constantly. At times I was criticized for being too humorous, too dark, *or* not being gloomy enough. At one event in Seattle, a young woman actually leapt from her chair because I had said the offensive word "lady." And years later, when speaking in the same area, I struck another raw nerve by having the audacity to utter the words "God bless." One person lit into me because I said the phrase six times. "Six times, in ninety minutes!" she screeched. I tried to genuinely apologize, for I was only trying to be respectful to the audiences, yet I was fuming for chasing yet someone else's needless approval.

I thought about my volunteer work as well. Since well before I started my business, I had always prided myself on assisting a cause. And because I could literally be any place at any time throughout the country, my office started an "in the area" file, which meant if I was going to a gig or a book signing, I could drop by whatever organization had requested me, gratis. But doing that became a quagmire. What began as a one-hour in-the-area radius, quickly became two hundred miles or more. One individual fumed because I was unable to visit his group home even though he was more than three hundred miles from where I had just done some volunteer work. (The same person later admitted he had never spoken to anyone in the office requesting a visit in the first place.)

My efforts in donations never seemed to be enough. When I had read about a family that took in children with extreme needs, I sent off a check to pay for a much-needed additional wing for their home. I was proud that my business was in the position to do something that could make a difference. I wanted the couple to *feel* that they were appreciated for their amazing service. But in less than a month, a man from the home phoned asking for more help. So, filling my need to please, I immediately sent out another check. But then, every week or so, there seemed to be another crisis that only my assistance could instantly solve. Months later, my office severed the relationship when the individual became unhinged when I did not overnight another donation for the purchase of another new car.

When it came to those matters, I believed my intention was *never* about chasing approval. It was simply trying to make others happy.

I knew exactly how lucky I was. Once, while in foster care, my aunt and uncle—for no reason—mailed me a card that included a crisp five-dollar bill. I still remember that newly printed smell when I brought the bill to my nose. I never forgot how that gesture made my heart soar, knowing that *I* meant that much to someone.

So, once a year before Christmas, I sent out personal checks to various friends and relatives as a symbol of sincerity. Admittedly, I did so in part out of guilt for all the time squandered and the immense misery some of us had been subjected to as kids. But my main reasoning was I knew that *I* had been so blessed while others, who might have been through far worse and worked just as hard, couldn't catch a break.

I always felt it was the right thing to do.

Yet, I knew that some viewed my generosity as a sign of complete gullibility. I didn't really mind. But over a period of years when one relative publicly ridiculed me, including on disturbing blogs on the Internet, it was hard for me to take another late-night phone call begging me for additional help as this person's home was about to enter foreclosure, again.

So, like in every situation, I did my best to think it through and pray for the right answer. Part of my problem was the rare commodity of time. Funds were always needed in a matter of mere hours. So, in the end, my guilt justified my assistance because my relative had kids and I didn't want them to go without as I had.

It became a treadmill. Just hours ago I'd had a fax in front of me from the same frustrating individual. It read: "It is my understanding that Dave wishes to make this year's donation to a charity rather than to our family.

"We had hoped that we would continue to be a part of what Dave has done over the years. It sounds like Dave no longer has that desire, at least not for my family.

"We have come to look forward to Dave's donations/ assistance. I hope that this will be reconsidered."

As I read, then reread, the correspondence, I could feel myself becoming unglued. But, like always, I kept it all inside.

In my sleep-deprived, weakened state, I announced to no one, "I don't deserve *this*!

"I'm good enough to dole out the bucks, but not good enough to even have this particular fax addressed to me?"

I replayed all the arguments Marsha and I had had over the same subject, dozens upon dozens of times. As my anger got the best of me, I could feel acid from my stomach rise. I stumbled from my office and into my bathroom. I made it in the nick of time.

A short time later, after washing my mouth and sweaty face and trying to relax my strained throat, I returned to the main office. I was so livid that I didn't want to explain anything to either Gabbi or Rey. I placed an envelope in the palm of Rey's hand. With all the energy I had left, I muttered, "Mr. Thayne, if it's not too much trouble, would you be so kind as to mail this for me? And if you would, can you make it overnight? Thank you, sir."

Before my executive director, Gabbi, could launch into me, I again fled to the safety of my bathroom. While clutching the toilet bowl, my hypercomputing mind fired off the frantic thought that I had to make sure I moved monies from one account to another so my *assistance* wouldn't bounce.

Hours later, as the last beams of the sun faded behind the mountains, my head still throbbed. My mind kept spinning.

Throughout my entire life, I had always felt, in part because of my feelings of inadequacy, that I had been teetering on a tightrope—I was never good enough, and at the same time I could never do enough!

I wanted to scream, to let out all the frustration and even hatred I kept in my lead-lined "lockboxes." I felt the same sense of anger as I had when I sat on my hands in the basement as The Family lived their lives upstairs. And, if only for a moment, just like back then, I was able to numb my pain, providing a layer of protection from feeling anything.

And now, nothing was working. I was done.

While trying to focus on the majestic beauty of my outside surroundings, I could still taste the bile from the bottom part of my throat. After more than forty years, I was disgusted by my results of *swallowing*.

"Screw this!" I snapped. At that moment, I could not escape my life fast enough.

CHAPTER 9

A PURPOSE WITH REDEMPTION

I KNEW THE IDEA OF FLEEING was another form of copping out, but obviously nothing in my life was working. In my zombie-like state during one of my midnight walks, I came to believe the toxic fax from my grifter relative should be looked on as a mixed blessing. As I was fighting to clear my swirling thoughts, I decided maybe *that* was the sign that I had been praying for.

Regardless of how it might have looked to anyone else, I felt it was time for me to do something radical. So, within a couple of days, I had two bags packed, bank accounts reshuffled, and a checklist I revised as often as once an hour.

As much as I tried to keep my intentions covert, I began to feel that Gabbi and Rey knew something was going on. What they might have interpreted as me being more withdrawn than normal was me busily prepping for my possible departure.

My SUV was spotlessly clean and topped off with gas. My bills were all paid in full for at least a month, and every piece of clothing I had was washed, folded, and properly placed—I could do no more. I felt like I was back in the military, waiting for the final deployment order. Back then I learned to adapt hour by hour. But now *I* was the sole person in charge of my fate.

I had fully planned my exodus. I would leave after five in the evening, just before sunset, and drive all night to Northern California, arriving before sunrise the next day. As doltish as it seemed, I clung to the sentimental notion of beginning my new life with a brand-new day.

There was only one place for me to go. As much as I adored Carmel-by-the-Sea and the expansive Monterey area, I knew *I* could never live there. I felt that I wasn't worthy enough to reside in such a unique community against the ocean. So, I justified, I would return to the redwood-filled town of Guerneville. As a child, I had always longed to live where my family vacationed, before the madness took hold. Later, it had been my saving grace when I fought to disconnect from the torture and isolation. By closing my eyes and slowing my breathing, I'd mentally transport myself to the majestic setting of the Russian River.

Years earlier, when Stephen's mother, Patsy, and I divorced, I had finally fulfilled my life-long desire to live at the summer river resort. It was then that I discovered how radically different, physically and psychologically, I was from the individuals who seemed proud of their ability to get by solely through public assistance and various levels of bartering.

To me, the naturalistic beauty and strong ties from my past had outweighed the stigma of what many outsiders dubbed "Grudge-ville." Even though at times I had felt I was making a huge mistake, in my own deep-rooted, and even romantic sense, the small river town *still* had a powerful connection to the best days of my childhood shared with both my parents.

In one instance, when I was six, I quietly followed my towering, reserved father when he went out for his after-dinner walk. I had, against the rules and ever so quietly, followed his footsteps, right up until the moment he spun around and discovered me. I flinched, imagining my father's retaliation. But in a blink of his kind black eyes, I knew all was well and that *I*, "the problem child," "the bad boy," was allowed to capture my father's undivided attention. At that time, as the wounds between Mother and me only festered, that rare moment with Father meant absolute security and love. It was the one memory I fought so hard to dream about until I had recently allowed Mother to invade my fantasy world.

It was during that same summer that another unexpected incident happened. One evening, as Ron, Stan, and I stood with eyes wide and mouths gaped open as the sun set behind the swaying redwood trees, against the majestic blue-orange skyline, I felt something brush up from behind me. It only took a few moments for me to accept that Mother had deliberately leaned down and wrapped her arms around me as she pulled me into her chest. She then whispered a sweet sentence for my ears only. Aside from one other summer vacation at Memorial Park, during which Mother and I had sat on the end of a decaying log fishing together, the remainder of my memories of Mother were filled with a blend of raging terror and absolute loneliness.

But even more than thirty-five years later, those rare moments of tenderness still held major sway in my heart.

Maybe Guerneville simply represented solace.

By moving back to the Russian River, I could return to the unpretentious condo complex and, because of the area's low expenses, simply retire. By calling it quits, there would be no more flights, no more getting up at one or two in the morning. No more spending the majority of my time on the road at all hours of the day. And the best thing would be that I'd be closer to my son.

I could, in my own way, become like many of those who fled to Guerneville (as if they were the new century's version of Steinbeck's *Cannery Row*), drop out and escape from general society and its woes. I could stop, completely stop running and devote my time, my energy, to *me*.

As my mind began to spool up, I enhanced my rationalization. The house in Rancho Mirage was way too big for one person and was still filled with memories of my failed marriage. And even though I had several *friends* for whom I had bought drinks and cigars, I (deliberately) really wasn't all that close to anyone.

But even after more than a week and a couple of out-and-back work trips, I still couldn't pull the trigger. Deep down, as much as I wanted to flee my sadness, I was too scared to make a change. I still clung to the overwhelming need for that one final sign.

I prayed. I kept my heart open, but nothing emerged. One afternoon, frustrated in the solitude of my darkened office, I thought since there was no signal for me to stay, maybe *that* in itself was the message that my time and efforts were no longer needed.

When I exhaled and opened my eyes, I could see my assistant, Rey, entering the room. By the look of his strained face, I knew something was horribly wrong.

"We have a situation." Rey presented me a page of notes as he stood over me to brief me in further detail. With every sentence I read, I could feel my stomach tighten. The more Rey explained, the more nervously I bit my lower lip.

After Rey finished, neither of us uttered a word. From across my office, I could hear the distinctive ticking sound from the German cuckoo clock I had purchased so many years ago, just after my mother passed away. As a child, when I sat at the bottom of the basement stairs shaking from the cold, there were countless times that I would concentrate on the faint echo of the relaxing, repetitive rhythm from above. I never told anyone how years later, when I was young, married, with a child and broke, what lengths I went through to obtain my awkward tribute to my past.

I quickly snapped out of my trance. "My Lord, three kids, in six months? And the last one…?"

"Enlisted. Age nineteen, just returned from AOR.* Spotless record. Clean-cut kid. Doesn't drink, but after he receives a Dear John letter, gets hammered, jumps on his motorcycle, races down the street, full throttle and… let's go."

"Jesus," I mumbled. "No chance of an accident?"

"No!" Rey firmly stated. "Kid told his friends that very night…"

* Military terminology for overseas hostile area of responsibility deployments.

"And why didn't his *friends* tell anyone?" I spewed.

Maintaining his composure, Rey simply inserted, "One of his friends did just that—phoned the military police. Just happened too quick. Kid rode off before the cops knew anything."

I lashed out, "This PTSD is going to be a big issue. If folks don't get a handle on it now, it's gonna bite 'em in the future…" Rey leaned over, giving me an odd look. "So," I deflected, waiting for the other shoe to drop, "where do we fit in?"

"Remember when you were traveling to all those bases?" Rey said, reminding me of how I'd visited seven military bases in just over two weeks in the middle of a month-long book tour. "This was one of the bases." Rey then flashed me one of his rare sarcastic grins. "Your mission is to drop by the base, as you will happen to be 'in the area.'"

Before my insecurity took hold, Rey plowed on. "You're ex-military, they know you, they trust you. They need someone to help these troops make that initial connection. You can help put them on the path, help get them on their way. You're a perfect fit."

I recalled my years as an in-flight refueling boom operator. Whenever a series of planes crashed, the higher-ups brought in some do-gooder touchy-feely *expert* to buck us up. At the time, we knew it was well-intended, but it still rubbed some of us the wrong way. "This kinda takes us way off the reservation," I challenged. "I'm no shrink. I'm just now coming to terms that if anybody's got issues…" I caught myself. "Hell, man, I just don't want to screw up."

"How can you?" he asked, trying to get me to bite. "Now the good news. This is all below the radar. Again, you happen to be in the area. They can't even pay expenses. And they need you as soon as you can get there."

"Rey, I'm not qualified for this. This is just a Band-Aid. It ain't going to change anything."

Reminding me that he was a former professional nurse with years of intense experience in matters of life and death, Rey jumped in, "I don't need to tell you of all people how sometimes *that* bandage, that one gesture of kindness, is just what a person needs until they can get to professional help, otherwise they just may bleed out. And without help, some people lose their life's protein quick," he emphasized with a snap of his fingers. "And others, well, they waste a lifetime bleeding out from their past, drop by drop and day by day." He slowly ended with a nod. "To do nothing, to turn away when there's a need..."

I fought my insecurity. I understood Rey's true meaning.

Giving me a brotherly smile, Rey said, "I'll make the arrangements." He turned to walk away, but after only a couple of steps, he stopped to add, "You really should trust yourself more. You've been doing this for years."

"I'm gonna come off as an asshole," I fired back, still feeling totally unqualified.

In another rare moment of humor, Rey stated in a bold tone, "That's why it's not called 'mission difficult.'"

A short time later I found myself standing in front of the famed Bethesda Naval Hospital, breathing heavily. After having completed my task at the Northern Military Air Force Base, Gabbi, on behalf of her husband, Aaron, had asked if I would consider stepping out of my box even further by visiting some of the wounded marines who had suffered extreme injuries in Iraq and Afghanistan.

Feeling insecure, I had whined like a little schoolboy. "I've never done my thing in a hospital before. What if I say or… or do something stupid?"

"No doubt you will!" Gabbi retorted. "How many times have you said, have you justified over all these years, that you go where needed 'cause it's the right thing to do?' Well, *I am telling* you, *this* is the right thing.

"You talk a lot about people needing to not live their lives in fear. To not be a prisoner to their past, about stepping up and stepping out. Well, I'm asking you to do just that. Action. Words. Deeds. This is you.

"Okay, so, your personal life's in the crapper. Stop being so self-centered. You're not the first and you certainly won't be the last. You've been given a gift. You can go anywhere at any time and help ease pain. Just dig deep and you'll find your way."

Gabbi's words still echoed as I passed through the sliding glass doors of the hospital entrance. Trapped in a fog, I tried to snap out of my cluttered head as two immaculately dressed marines stepped forward in their distinctive olive-green uniforms to greet me. Both men wore row upon row upon yet another row of combat ribbons. The two marines briefed me as we walked toward the elevators.

For a few moments, the three of us remained silent as the elevator rose. As civilians entered and left on various floors, I noticed how the two marines gave a respectful nod to every one of them. "My God," I said to myself, "these guys are the real deal. Duty, honor, country!" Suddenly years of doubting myself over my little oddities—saluting my flag, being courteous to others, giving my all, committing to a cause—began to melt away. For the first time in a long, long time, I began to feel a quiet but nurturing resolve.

As the doors opened on our floor, I replayed a silent prayer that I had said thousands of times. "Heavenly Father, please grant me strength, give me courage, use me as your vessel. And please, please, please, I beg of you, don't let me screw this up."

The captain leaned toward me. "I need for you to understand, some of these men were airlifted from their FOBs.* One day they're in the field pulling an op, and the next they wake up back in the States. It's a lot for them to process."

"Yes, sir," I said, remembering some of my military experiences. "I can understand."

"Another thing that's mission critical," the captain advised, "no matter what you see in these units, *you* don't flinch. You don't show these marines anything that may make them feel bad about themselves. You hold it in, you bury it, you disconnect."

"That, I can do," I affirmed.

"Heard that 'bout you," the captain said with a wry smile. "Got a full sit rep** from your office."

We came to the first room. "Okay, it's go time," the captain said.

The sergeant reached into a box of my books, which had been shipped days before along with dozens of the

* Forward operating bases.

** Situation report.

commemorative coins that I had designed years ago, and which I had presented to thousands of service members.

One side of the coin showed an air force air tanker, like the kind I had flown on years ago, midair refueling the SR-71 Blackbird. On the flip side it displayed an American flag surrounded by the words "IN GRATITUDE FOR SACRIFICE WITH HONOR" around the border.

I reached out to retrieve a coin and a couple of books. The captain leaned in. "Composure," he warned. "Flip the switch." Again I nodded before opening the heavy door. The two other men remained behind.

Before my eyes could adjust, the first thing that hit me was that distinctive scent of sterile cleanliness. It immediately brought me back to when my father had died in my arms after his long battle with cancer of the neck and throat. He passed away a skeleton of his former self and without being able to utter a single syllable. I'd detested hospitals after that. Hospitals were to me what Kryptonite was to Superman.

Suddenly I felt completely overwhelmed, as if some invisible weight had crash-landed on my shoulders. My mind cried out, "What in the *hell* do you think *you're* doing?"

The more my lungs took in the air, the more lightheaded I became. I could feel my right foot begin to slip as my head and eyes rolled backward. By sheer luck, I grabbed the handle to the door. A moment later my eyes adjusted to the marine sitting up in his bed. He must have sensed my nervousness. Without skipping a beat, the young man quipped, "You should *so* see the other guy!"

His one-liner was the perfect icebreaker. In less than a minute, I found myself sitting on his bed cracking a few off-color jokes. I then slowed the tempo, asking about the young man's past, his family, and his future plans. Without hesitation, the Midwest-raised nineteen-year-old stated, "Just want to get back in there."

I nodded, trying to absorb his words and inner strength.

"I'm gonna get better. This," he pointed to his injuries, "this ain't nothing but a *thing*. This will soon pass. Like they say in basic, *mind over matter*. I don't mind 'cause—"

"This shit doesn't matter," I said, finishing the sentence that military instructors had used since the beginning of time to encourage, cajole, and sometimes threaten service members to take their internal capabilities to the next level.

After we shared a laugh, I could feel the young marine withdraw. "I'm not out of it. I'm gonna get better."

I jumped off his bed and reached in my pocket for a coin. "No doubt."

"You really think so?" His eyes lit up.

I then stood perfectly erect and palmed the marine's hand with the coin. "On behalf of a grateful nation, my office, and my family, words can never express my gratitude for your sacrifice and courage."

Moments later, with my hand on the door, the young lad yelped out, "Keep the faith!"

I stopped, pivoted, and then saluted the marine. "Always."

The first thing I noticed after closing the door behind me was the hallway's temperature—a degree or two warmer. As if I had become hypersensitive, my eyes seemed to focus on objects faster and with more clarity. Exhaling, I stood still. I could feel my head clear itself of all the needless white noise that constantly seemed to dominate my thoughts—fear, insecurity, hopelessness, unworthiness, abandonment, and above all, the deadening crucifix of shame.

Passing me a bottle of water, the marine sergeant asked, "So, how was it?"

Normally before anyone could finish a sentence, I was ready to fire off a nervous, comical retort. Now, I could not come up with the words to describe the very intimate experience. I swallowed the water, feeling it roll down my throat. I squinted at both men, who eyed me carefully. "Gentlemen, all I could think of..." I tried to allow myself to slow down. To feel. To be extremely careful not to open *that* locked door to my emotions. "...are the words, 'what an honorable privilege.'"

"So," the captain hesitated, "you're okay? You don't mind?"

"*Mind?*" I asked myself. "Why the hell should it bother me?"

The three of us began to walk down the hallway.

Quietly the captain stated, "Seeing these marines brings the cost of one's war home. It can challenge a person to truly look deep within themselves..."

"Yeah," I agreed.

"Makes you question your values, your priorities... your whole life's purpose," the sergeant broke in.

"Then," the captain chimed, "there are those, the Joe Hollywood types, who clamor to come here for a 'hey, look at me, I care' photo op. Then they run for the hills after seeing a single marine. All the while blubbering how hard it is *for them*."

Without knowing why, I found myself taking a half step back as if I had suddenly lost my balance. I also found myself blinking uncontrollably.

Fighting to recover, all I could do was exhale, processing how, ever so slowly, day by day, situation by situation, I had become completely self-absorbed. Thinking only of how situations affected poor little me! Suddenly, I was ashamed of my own skin.

"So," I asked, clearing the mechanism in my head, "the corporal back there, is he going to be okay?"

The two marines looked at each other before the captain quietly replied, "He's to be medically discharged. He's having a hard time coming to terms. He's still between denial and anger. He's nowhere near acceptance. It's sad, the corps is the only family he's really had. Came from a broken home... was abused, ran away... placed in foster care... a few scrapes with the law... we get a lot of that."

I sighed, thinking of how dedicated the kid was as compared to so many adults I personally knew who never contributed to any cause while blaming their life's failures on others and still demanded everything for themselves.

"So what do we have next?" I gently probed.

Both men quietly gave me the rundown. By midmorning the two marines and I developed our own rhythm. Before entering the rooms, the captain and sergeant gave me particulars on names, ranks, hometowns, injuries, and even what kind of movies or music the marines liked, which I was able to use as an icebreaker. And, with every visit, spending anywhere from five to thirty minutes per marine, I felt so damn lucky, after all I'd been through, to simply to have ten fingers and ten toes.

One young man jumped out of his bed. "Do you remember coming to my school, three, four years ago? In Modesto? That continuation school back at Cali?"

For the life of me I could not recall. In the past four years I had literally been to hundreds upon hundreds of schools. But the young man's eyes were hungry for recognition.

"Yeah," I lied, shaking my head slowly. I switched gears. "So, how are we today?"

"Okay. Just chilling. Lost my arm," the marine casually stated as he demonstrated by turning his shoulder.

"Well, hell, son, let's go find it!"

The young man laughed, and I pulled up a seat next to his bed so we could talk. We rambled about our lives, unexplained twists of fate, and how to deal with the next challenging episode on our paths.

"So, one question," the marine began to ask. "All that shit as a kid, how did you do it?"

"Okay," I blinked, "here's the real deal. Truth be told, I just did what I had to do. One step, one hour, one op, one meal at a time. Just like you, marine."

"But," the marine interrogated, "you still got *it*, right?" He emphasized by pounding the middle of his chest.

I sat back, stunned by the simplistic depth of his question. As I pondered my answer, the injured man continued to stare through my eyes.

"I have... I, ah, live this different life. Travel all the time, always on the road, never at home..."

"Tell me about it!" the marine stated.

"Well, at least for a while now, it seems I got my head wrapped around the wrong axle. I screwed up. I keep screwing up. At the worst of it, when I'm down in that hole looking up at that light to show me the way out, knowing all the time it's going to be a bitch to climb out of this thing, thinking how tired I am, how I don't have the strength, how unfair life can be—well, I try my best to flush all that shit away. 'Cause at the end of the day, no matter what, the thing that still pulls me out of every, and I mean every situation, is *if I could do all that shit as a kid without a lot of help or training, I can damn well do anything*!"

"Yeah, man!" the marine stated. "I know what you mean. You gotta have that inner core."

"And you have it son, *you* have it. Otherwise you wouldn't have made it this far. The corps is *your* core."

The young man began to cry. On the outside, I maintained my composure waiting for him to say something first.

"Had to lose it to really feel her," the marine blindly said as he slightly moved his shoulder above where his arm used to be.

Feeling his immense pain made an ice-cold chill shoot up my spine.

"As a kid, I used to give my ma so much crap. When Pops took off, I blamed my ma. And no matter what, no matter what time she came home from work, sometimes late at night, she'd always hug me. You know, the two-arm, double-barrel hug. Even when we fought, and I said things, 'cause I was hurting inside, she'd always sit by my bed and try to lift me up and hug me. By the time I was in high school, I tried to stick it to her. I'd act like I was sleeping and shake her off. I did that a lot. She never knew.

"I hated her when she was gone at work, and couldn't wait for her to come home. Then, when Ma came home, I couldn't wait for her to leave. I made her life hell." The marine stopped as if to collect his thoughts. "You know, I joined the corps to get away.

"Anyhow, day comes when I'm going to basic. I got my crew with me, and Ma wants to do the Ma thing, so I shake her off before she can give me a hug, so I don't look like some momma's boy… now look at me. I lost…" The young man's voice trailed off in midsentence.

"You didn't lose a damn thing," I interjected. "You have the best blessing of all—your mother's unconditional love."

The marine nodded as a stream of tears began to trickle down his face. Easing off, we talked about matters of no importance. I made sure I cracked a few jokes before I gave him some books and presented him with a coin. We held hands for an extra second that seemed to matter to both of us.

"Guess I had to lose my arm to find her love. Now when I hug her, I can really feel her. Just like when I was a kid. Just don't know how to say I'm sorry for all those years I gave her so much shit."

"She knows, son. She knows. She's proud of you. By hugging her *now* and not letting go… well, that tells her everything."

Stepping out of the room, I had to stop in the hallway to collect myself. As the day went on, with each visitation, it seemed I was taking longer to recover from each experience. I saw and felt so much pain that had little to do with the actual physical traumas those brave young men had experienced.

"All right," the captain broke in, "this one's a live wire, always pulling pranks on his squad. You should do well with this one. Get in there!"

A second later I burst into the room firing off several rounds of jokes without letting up. It wasn't until the young man lifted up the side of his gown that I discovered my mistake. From the middle of his right thigh to the side portion of his chest, silver metal staples ran the length of his body like tiny railroad tracks.

"Hey, I'm so sorry," I apologized as I approached the side of his bed. "I kinda get ahead of myself."

"No worries." The marine readjusted himself in his bed.

I asked if I could sit on the side of the young man's bed. He kindly agreed, then told me how he felt about being medically discharged.

"I could man a desk. Maybe even become an instructor, telling the newbies what it's like out there." The private stopped himself, shaking his head as if he had already come to terms and was simply venting one last time. "I know it ain't gonna happen. If anything, I can finally go to college. You know, settle down. Kinda felt I was putting off lots of stuff, not doing what's best for me. I don't mean the corps, mind you, but other things." The marine reached up to pull himself up by gripping a triangle-shaped device above his head.

"What things?" I asked, sensing the young man wanted to open up further.

"Well," his faced became flushed, "there's this girl."

I nodded. "Always is. You're not in trouble?" I asked, suddenly feeling like the young man's uncle.

"Oh, hell no! It's not like that at all. Anyhow, we were supposed to get married. Bought her the ring. It wasn't a big rock like you see in them movies, but it took six months to pay for. But now that this happened," he pointed to his side, "she won't even see me. Been here over three weeks. I told her I'd spring for the plane ticket and everything else, but now, she won't even take my calls. I gotta call her friends just to snag her for a sec. When I call her folks, it's like she's always 'out.'" He used his two hands to emphasize the last word.

"Do you love her?" I directly asked.

"Well?" He exhaled as though his batteries had just been drained. "Yeah… kinda. Sure, yeah."

"You either do or you don't. You're either a marine *or* you're not! Do *you* love *this* girl?"

"Here's the thing," he began, but I already knew the answer.

"Lying in this bed," the marine continued to confess, "spending all this time alone, without mags, music, or DVDs, it really makes you think. Makes you, really forces you, to put things in perspective. Anyhow, I knew she went out with me in part 'cause of the uniform. And she knew I knew. I was okay with it, at first. Kinda thought she'd learn to like me for me. But then after a while."

"Four to six months?" I asked.

"Yeah! How'd you know?"

"Trust me, it's perfectly normal. Go on."

"Well, it was like she got on my case all the time 'bout me, my clothes, my car, how officers, even sergeants, made more dough. My work schedule: training rotations, shift work, predeployment stuff. Even 'bout going to church." He stopped to shake his head. I could tell he was on a different tangent. "Think about it, man. She's a stay-at-home, one-semester community college dropout, daddy's girl. Too good to even work at the mall or flip a burger. All that free time and she's bustin' my balls about me going to church."

I didn't dare shake my head. I didn't want to stop the young man's flow. I knew exactly that taking all that unneeded crud stemmed from his own feelings of unworthiness. The marine probably believed that he could never do any better. I figured the girl knew it and simply worked everything to her advantage. After hearing about the church statement, I almost blurted, "Jesus!" Thankfully, for once, I kept my big trap shut.

"Anyhow, we fought a lot. Nothing serious, just jabs here and there. Break up, make up. So, anyway, I'm thinking, she's gonna want to dump me when I deploy, so..."

"So you got engaged!"

"Yeah." He nodded. "All the while, I'm thinking, man, if I just do this thing, this *one thing*, I'll show her, if she'll let me, I can prove to her."

"If you can *fix it*. Then everything will fall into place and the two of you will live happily ever after in Fairy Tale Land, right?" I inserted.

"I know. I know. Dit, dee, dee," the young man rang out. "Everybody said the same thing. I know. It's just, I just thought, it would be different. That... I could, you know."

His eyes began to well up. He was so close.

"Say it!" I said in a low but commanding voice. "Go ahead, *you* need to hear your own words. Give yourself permission. Open up and just frickin' say it!"

"All right!" He almost shouted, "*I* thought if I could just fix it, it would fix her. That it would fix us! Okay? I get it!" he snapped more at himself than at me.

I could hear the muffled sounds of carts scurrying back and forth in the hallway. I reached out to touch the young man's arm. "I mean no disrespect," I said, "but this gal, she ain't for you!"

He gave me a meek nod.

"You want to serve, while she's all about being served. You're a young man, she's still a self-absorbed child. Love's about growing together. About giving yourselves to each other. And for now, no matter what you do, it will never be enough. She's not even thinking of trying to make you happy, let alone coming out to see you in your time of need."

"She, well, she said that seeing me, like this, would be too hard for *her*."

"What?" I asked, not sure what I just heard. "Come back. Say again?" I reverted back to military jargon.

"Too hard. Too hard for her," the marine replied, not sure of my inquiry.

"The hell you say." Suddenly, I flashed back. In perfect clarity I could see myself when I was just nineteen, standing in front of my mother in my rumpled air force fatigues after coming straight from the field, flying all night so I could go to the hospital where my father, her still-not-divorced husband, sat in a bed rotting away from cancer. When I somehow summoned the guts to ask why, after more than four months, she still had not visited him, she immediately put on the waterworks, complete with a high-pitched, strained voice, proclaiming for all the world to hear that seeing him would be too hard for *her*.

Even though I had not stepped foot in that house for more than seven years, I still was under her controlling influence. And, even though I had begun to make my own way, and had already accomplished a fair amount against a few odds, in Mother's presence, I was still that child called "It." I wanted to beg Mother, the good Mother of long, long ago, just to see my father, her onetime love. And maybe, somehow, wipe that slate of hatred she carried clean and send Father off with love.

Back then, I would have made a deal with the devil himself.

Hearing that phrase almost twenty five years later made my blood boil. If she were still alive today, I would have taken Mother at gunpoint if needed. I would have made her put on a nice dress, do the whole hair and makeup routine, my father's favorite perfume, and march her over to Dad's room and make damn sure she stayed by his side to the very end.

I shook my head, fighting to clear my thoughts. "Sorry, excuse me. I'm just saying that's not right. That's all."

"So then, she's gone?" he asked.

"Brother," I let out a nervous laugh. "She was never there," I said, pointing to his heart. "Consider it a blessing. If you got hitched, or God forbid had kids, it would have only gotten worse."

"Man, I know," he confessed. "I know. But what now?"

Without breaking stride I jumped in with more military lingo. "Recover! Get well. Get strong. Get better. *Know better, do better.*

"Can't believe I'm saying this, must be my age, but you really need to hear this—you're a young man and *you will* find the one. The *right* one! And when you do, watch out. She will so rock your world.

"I'm talking about when the outside world is nothing but a constant, massive storm of shit, and you two can still find that certain peace in each other's arms in the middle of that long, dark, ice-cold night. When you both know that through thick and thin, you're there for each other. Well then, that's the juice, that's the high. That's the real deal. And at night, when she rolls over and kisses you on the face or shoulder *while* she's still deep asleep you'll think you died and gone to heaven." My voice trailed off.

The young man sat back with a wide smile on his face. "You certainly know women." He smiled while looking at my wedding band.

I shook my head before explaining the hard truth. "I'm kinda what you call damaged goods. What I know about women is not too much. For me, it's too little, too late."

As I left, we both leaned in to give each other a hug. I could tell that he would spend a fair amount of time processing his future, especially after he asked, "Where'd you fly in from?"

Not sure of his intention, I stammered, "Cali. Palm Springs area."

"How many flights?"

"Two, no, three flights. No big deal." I knew where he was going. I knew he was still thinking about that girl not making the effort.

"So, why'd *you* come?"

With my hand on the door, I declared, "Outta respect, son. That's why!"

The young man beamed.

Locking eyes, I fired off one last piece of advice, "Above all, never, ever, forget *your* worth."

Closing the door behind me, I stopped midstride and I thanked God.

The sergeant leaned over and gave me a tissue, while using his other hand to point at his eye. "You may wanna...?"

I hadn't even noticed. I turned and walked down the hallway, waiting for the two marines to join me. By the time we met up the tension seemed to subside. My internal circuit breaker was still flipped.

As the three of us strolled back and forth in the long hallway, I noticed how none of us spoke for the longest time. I also observed how we seemed to slow our pace when we approached one particular door.

"All right." The captain leaned in while looking at his sergeant. "Here's the deal, we can call it a day, or you can visit this one last marine?"

"It's up to you," the sergeant added.

I could feel something was up. "Okay, what gives?"

The captain flipped open his chart. "Marine's a corporal. Inside are both parents, his wife, and newborn baby... girl... eight months old. And..." The captain stumbled. "Sergeant, would you give Mr. P. the sit rep?"

"Yes, sir," the marine chirped. "Before sustaining injuries while in the field, his boot camp buddy was shot and killed right in front of him. Then, his platoon sergeant was killed by an IED[*] twenty-four hours later, while he in was in the same vehicle. Two days later, the corporal was shot."

"My God," I gasped. "Are you telling me, all this... all this happened in a period of"—I stopped while calculating the hours—"four days?"

"We computed all events transpired in less than ninety hours," the sergeant stated.

I looked at both men, knowing there was something else. "And?"

"He's Catholic," the younger of the two marines said.

The captain grunted slightly while looking over his shoulder as if to check that no one could eavesdrop. "A nurse checks in on him every fifteen minutes."

"Are you telling me he's on—"

The captain gave me a cold, hard stare. "No. Mr. Pelzer, *I* am not saying anything of the kind."

The sergeant looked at the captain, then back at me. "I understand," I exhaled.

"He's just been through a lot," the captain said, giving me a pat on my shoulder. "You have to realize that we're here to protect and support our brothers in their time of need."

"Got it, Capt," I replied. "I meant no disrespect."

"None taken." The captain smiled. "Want a sit rep on his medical status?" I nodded, and continued to do so with every sentence both men gave out. Without realizing it, I still was shaking my head ever so slightly after the two marines finished.

"I know this is a lot." The sergeant tried to soften. "Maybe too much."

[*] Incendiary explosive device.

Suddenly, I felt slighted. I caught myself before I could imagine Mother standing in the busy hallway clamoring for everyone's attention and sympathy. I swallowed hard while flushing the thought away. "Imagine what it's like for him," I announced to no one.

The first thing that caught my attention upon entering the quiet room was the darkness, as if I had just stepped into a long tunnel. With the blinds closed, only a couple of soft lights were lit in the front of the room, and none by the bedside.

The next thing I picked up on was the sudden coldness, reminding me of my early days in the air force when I worked as a cook in the field. I would enter the freezer storage and feel that instant drop in temperature; it was so cold that I could see the white vapor escaping my mouth. I thought I picked up an odd smell. The scent made me think of my father just before he passed away.

I blinked my eyes as if to reset my inner switch. "For God's sake," I yelled at myself, fighting to get my mother out of my head. "*This* is not about you! Man up!"

A second later, I broke through with a wide smile and introduced myself to the nervous wife, who rocked her sleeping baby in her slender arms. I shook hands with the marine's gracious mother and father. After paying my respects and signing a few books for the wife, I sat next to the marine, who sat in a wide chair next to a table.

Out of respect and not to draw any unwanted attention, I deliberately did not look at his face until the young man poked my arm and lifted his chin as if to give me permission.

Hearing someone read off a chart that this poor lad had been literally shot in the face and had already endured seven operations, with more to go, was one thing. For me, seeing the results just a few inches away was quite another.

I knew that if I flinched even in the slightest—a nervous gasp, or even just a flutter of my eyes, it would have been taken as if *I* was offended. Instead, I pulled my glasses down to the tip of my nose and looked directly at the marine, who gave no hesitation to my quasi-inspection.

As the marine turned his head from left to right and up and down, I thanked God Almighty that the lead from the assailant's bullet hadn't spun up and into the young man's brain. Yet the damage was done. The right cheekbone was gone. All that I could see in its place was a light red square layer of gauze. I knew his jaw was wired and I could see the maze of tubes entering his body, but he looked good to me.

Readjusting my glasses, I thanked him for allowing me that close. With a stillness between us, it was then that I noticed the slight but raspy sound from the marine. He sat back in his chair as if waiting for something. I could see the wife and parents retreating ever so slightly as if to give the two of us more privacy.

Leaning into the side of his face, I whispered, "Are you in *any* pain?"

He slowly shook his head no, before rolling his eyes as if he had had too much to drink.

"Wanna sell me any of your meds?"

He indicated he got the joke by patting my knee and making a slight gurgling sound.

I leaned in closer, almost brushing my chin against his ear. "How we doin'?"

I had failed to notice the marine had a thick black marker in one hand, just above a yellow spiral notepad that rested on the table. With great effort, he wrote, "2 DY OK."

"Good," I whispered. "Good for you."

In a flash, his eyes filled with tears. A second later, he hit my leg as if to emphasize his point before writing, "DEAD. I LIVE BOTH DEAD DEAD DEAD."

As my eyes read the words, he drew circles around the words "DEAD," before X-ing out the words "I LIVE."

His pain was like a slow earthquake one could hear coming before the destructive force hit. I felt completely worthless. "I know. I know."

He bent toward the table. His hand shook as if he were shooing away some fly. It took him a few seconds as he strained to write in capital letters, "WHY."

Not understanding, I almost shook my head, before the marine added the word, "ME." After a swirl of circles around the last word, he dropped the marker. As the marker struck the table, for me, the reverberating sound might as well have been a crystal vase that had just shattered into a million pieces—it echoed into the deepest part of my heart.

For the young man the sound seemed to have the same effect. His chest seemed to heave. Not sure what to do, I turned toward his wife, who gave me a slight nod, as if to say, "Do something."

I turned back toward the marine. I had no words. I had absolutely nothing to give him.

For a fraction of a second, I blinked my eyes shut and prayed to myself, "Please, God."

A moment later, I just did what came naturally. In a fluid movement, I reached over and, as carefully as possible, I embraced the young man, who without hesitation fell into my arms.

I hugged the marine as if he were my own Stephen, when he was that preschool boy who came to me after he scraped himself from falling off his little red bicycle. I embraced the young man as I had so wanted to do with my father that one summer when we walked together in Guerneville. I held onto him as if he were the last person on earth.

In this rarest of opportunities a portal opened. "You have to release this pain," I whispered. "Why you? Your God has picked you for a reason. You survived, you are living because He has a plan for you. An entirely new mission for you.

"You have a wife, parents, and the responsibility of raising a baby. Your baby! To go against His will, after all you've suffered, that would be the worst sin of all." As I spoke with my eyes closed, I remembered seeing a rosary on the table beside his notepad.

"Your brothers are home. They are not in any pain. They love you. They will be with you always. They don't want you in any pain. They want you to be happy." I reached down, digging a bit further. "You survived. You did! It's an awesome responsibility to carry on, but you have to be ready for it. So, for now, right now... all you have to do is get well. Just breathe. Breathe in, absorb all the love. With every breath, I want you to draw in all the strength you can. Exhale all the impurities, anything that can weaken your faith."

I could sense I was getting through. I lowered my voice even more. "I don't know a lot. *But* I can only tell you in my heart what I know *is* true. This is not over yet. That for you, this *is* in fact, a new beginning. God's love for you saved you. You have a purpose. You survived so that others may *live*."

A short time later the two marines and I stood in the lobby where we first came together what seemed like a lifetime ago. I was beyond exhausted. Yet in my best protocol manner, I properly coined the two marines before I hugged them both. I was fully aware it wasn't the macho thing to do. Yet, me being me, I thought it was the right thing to do.

For so many years and so many reasons, or excuses, I had held back. Part of that cost was that gold band I continued to wear but needed to let go.

As I looked down at my left hand, I noticed my right hand beginning to twitch. Before I could form a fist to stop the shaking, the captain advised, "You should get that looked at."

I nodded, understanding the exact message he was giving me.

A couple of hours later, I sat outside my hotel gazing at the beauty that surrounded me. A few feet away, inside, happy hour was in full swing for the well-heeled road warriors of the Washington, DC, set. For a moment I found it odd that no one else took just a moment to sit and admire the multitude of flowers in all their brilliance.

Then I got it. "Always have and always will be the odd duck." I smiled at myself. I took a slow sip of red wine before reporting to Gabbi. After telling her how much I learned, how much I was given from the visit, she asked, "Are you okay?"

I looked again at the impatiens flowers, thinking how lucky I was, after all that I had been through, after all that *I* had been *given*. "Gabbi, *I'm* gonna be fine." I paused for a long moment before concluding, "It's only a divorce."

I then flipped the cell phone off. As I finished my wine, staring at the beauty around me, I gave a quick prayer of thanks. I could feel some of my anger slowly dissipate. As it did, I didn't have the energy to cry.

CHAPTER 10

THE BARGAINING BUREAU

EVEN THOUGH I WAS on an unexpected long path of introspection, after Bethesda, there was little doubt that I had a meaningful purpose. Alone in my darkened office I replayed the events, reconnecting to the roller coaster of my emotions. I realized how certain threads from my past could suddenly pull me in.

Drawing in a deep breath, I snatched the phone, and called the Rio Villa hotel at the Russian River, where I'd made plans to stay until I found my new home. I apologized about the sudden cancellation. "No worries," Ron, the innkeeper, chimed.

I swallowed hard, knowing I had to state the words for myself. "Can't do it," I choked. "I'm… *not* going to move. At least, not now. I just can't quit."

Ever understanding, my friend of many years replied, "*You* don't need to run." He then stopped as if to collect his thoughts. "I know this is hard, and I can't begin to tell you how many people I have known who have gone through a major loss—death, divorce, being laid off, you name it. Understandably they just want to throw up their hands and get the hell out of Dodge. It may work for a while, but in the end—"

I nodded into the receiver. "You can run away from everything and everybody, but you always end up with yourself."

"True. True. Besides," Ron added, "when you really think about it, are you sure that Guerneville's really for you? Is it what you really want?"

I already had major reservations about pouncing to that destination. I stumbled before I thanked Ron again and said good-bye.

I sat back in my high-back chair. I openly huffed to the empty room, "It's all I've ever known. It's all that I ever longed for." Digging a bit deeper, I honestly admitted, "It's all I ever fixated on."

The next day at the office, without coming out and openly revealing my near eleventh-hour exodus, I announced, "For as long as we can, for as long as God lets us, we're gonna carry on."

I had wanted to sound more astute, but inside I was still reeling over my recent visits with the military. After all I had been subjected to, and even with my latest personal trauma, I was still an extremely lucky, very blessed person. Now every time I reached over to answer a phone call, strolled through the cove, even watched TV, every little thing took on an appreciative meaning.

Slowly walking into my private office, I stopped and smiled at all the various items that still held a deep emotional connection to me. Upon entering, I could see the American and California flags proudly hung on dark wooden poles along the back wall, a mere fraction of the books that I had read and kept over twenty-five years, my air force flight suit, my son's flight jacket, which he had excitedly worn when he was just a preschooler, and the Olympic torch I had carried for the Centennial Games.

Yet of all things collected over the course of my life, and the millions of miles traveled, the one item that seemed completely out of place was what I dubbed The Stick. The gray, dried-out, nine-inch, jagged piece of wood was, to any typical person, anything but exceptional.

When I had recently brought The Stick home, I felt like Indiana Jones, who, after a perilous expedition, finally obtained some monumental, mystical, archaeological treasure. It was more than a thirty-five-year journey, and I was surprised how much I still carried, deep within my damaged heart, that rare, sacred moment of bonding with my mother during her depths of madness.

Yet before any emotion could bubble to the surface, I instantly locked the feeling into one of my decaying internal boxes.

I turned to my library. Without thinking, I plucked out a worn, blue-covered tome from the tightly squeezed row. I recalled how, as far back as my days as a petrified child, I'd used books as my very own bargaining chip, and how the tomes were a major thread during the course of my life.

As Mother's human punching bag, I had devised a way to use books as a protective barrier. Mother valued work assignments from school, thinking if I kept up with my homework, I could draw away any attention from the fact that I might be at risk. With all the courage I could muster, with my insides shaking, I had flat-out lied to Mother's distorted face, telling her that yes, because I was *so* slow, *so* stupid, and *so* pathetic, I had to write stacks upon stacks of book reports. Much to my surprise, she bought into it. I couldn't believe as cunning, as chess-like as Mother was when it came to her deviant premeditated torturous games, that I was in fact psychologically playing her.

But books were so much more than a covert shield. Back then, as I sat in the basement, I would strain my tired eyes to capture every word of every sentence. I digested endless books about turtles, alligators, volcanoes, and the occasional fictional stories of high adventure. Alone in the enveloping darkness I would at times shake from the cold and clamp my eyes shut. I'd then transport myself, imagining I was that cabin boy on a pirate ship, or stranded alone on a deserted island, or anyone else that I had read about. At times my imaginary world not only helped me escape the reality of my life, but more importantly, the pages gave me strength to keep me from collapsing into myself.

But while books were a form of escapism and my first token for bargaining, coming to terms with my real-life triggers was a substantial challenge for me. Ever since what I dubbed The Basement Days, as a safety mechanism, I had learned to take my pain, my shame, my *whatever* and heave it into boxes. If I was scared, I'd shut it down and put it in a box. If I felt threatened, while on the outside it appeared as if I was frozen or robotic, on the inside, faster than the speed of light, I'd shut down and throw my fear into the box. So, over time, whenever things turned south, when plans never amounted to anything, when relationships soured and trust became broken—everything went in the box.

And now, standing alone in my crammed, precisely shelved, orderly sanctuary with another loss under my belt, I stopped to examine the layers upon layers and rows upon rows of boxes I'd built inside me. In my mind, I had everything categorized, chronicled, and alphabetized. The *real* deep shame, the degrading, humiliating situations, those went into boxes *within* boxes. And the things I wanted to hide from God Himself, I hid those in the nontransparent, Superman-couldn't-even-see-through-lead boxes in the deepest recesses of my cerebral storage facility.

And yet I missed my father.

As much as I tried, as much as I repackaged, rearranged, and reshelved the death of my father, for no apparent reason, the loss was like a Jack-in-the-Box that would suddenly, painfully, and instantly pop up.

Of all the boxes, the one that I dared not unlock was *my* lie. Even though I had tried to live my life as an honorable person and do what I could to help others, I had in fact committed the worst of sins. I had not only lied to my own father, but I had deliberately lied to a dying man.

Back then, at the hospital, just a few miles from Father's fire station on Post Street, I selfishly did not want to let him go. *I* needed *him* for *me*. So, at his bedside, I painted the picture like a Monet piece of art for him of the future, coloring every aspect of the Russian River cabin that I had bought for him, for us, to live out our days together in peace and harmony.

I laid it on thick. I described the rounded, hand-carved wooden chairs placed on a circular worn rug in front of the glowing fireplace, the smooth river-stone chimney and even a small axe on a stump by the nearby woodpile. It was all set against the backdrop of the bright green ferns and the ever-present majestic redwoods.

Every word that spilled from my mouth, I felt like a stroke of my paintbrush. While I created the words, it somehow all perfectly fit into the frame that I had carried inside of me for all of my life.

In the end, I thought Father smiled. He knew. Even when he strained to lean up and kiss me good-bye, I had still selfishly wanted him to pull through, not only for himself, but for me and my idiotic fantasy. Above all, I craved a connection that we really never had.

While standing in front of my life's collections in my office, gazing down at The Stick in its own clear container, I thought, maybe now was the time, the opportunity to give myself permission to open some of my other hurt boxes.

CHAPTER 11

LOOKING

"SO... HOW YOU DOIN'?" Stephen's mother, Patsy, kindly asked during a late-night phone call.

"You know, good days, some bad ones, but now," I confessed, "it's more on the good side. I think I'm over the hump."

"Are you eating?"

"Every day." I sighed.

"And are you getting enough sleep?"

"It's getting better." I yawned.

"If I know you, you're probably running around, doing anything to stay busy—still cleaning your phone with a Q-tip?"

"Only once a day," I snarked back.

"Okay, I'll stop," Patsy said. "I just wanted to check on you and tell ya 'bout Steve-e-o."

Patsy and I exchanged tidbits about our son, who, like most young adults, would tell Patsy certain things about his life while sharing other elements with me.

"Can you believe that *our* boy is in college?" I asked, out of the wonder of the moment. "Holy Mother of God. We've both come a long ways, Pats. A long ways. Good on you."

Patsy took the compliment. She then resumed chatting, updating me on Stephen's adjustment to college life. With the phone pressed against my ear, I drifted into my office. I stopped in front of a photo of Stephen when he was about two years old, proudly sitting on my then-prized motorcycle. He was clad only in his bright green swimming trunks and beaming as only children at that wondrous age can.

Next to that photo was another one that showed Stephen a couple of years later, wearing his little flight jacket. He giggled with joy as Patsy leaned down to wrap the joy of our life in her arms in front of a waterfall during a rare trip to Golden Gate Park. I beamed back at the picture. Even after all the hell Patsy and I put each other through, in part due to our own fears and past experiences, I still cherished that moment in time.

Taking the framed picture, I sat down, stroking the photo with the tip of my finger. I recalled when my son was just a newborn baby, and how I used to measure Stephen's growth by the length of my lap. It truly seemed like only yesterday when Stephen was born.

Alone in my world while being overtaken with fatigue from my day's activities, with Patsy's voice in my ear, I thought about the road that led me to her.

It was May of '84 when my entire life changed.

By perseverance, prayers, and sheer luck, I had completed flight school. Part of my challenge was my never-ending, self-sabotaging mindset of informing myself, "I'm not worthy enough. I'm not smart enough. I don't deserve to be here." My tape-fed contamination led me to get behind in some of the fast-paced courses, which in turn almost brought me to the edge of flunking out. Then one early morning while driving to the flight line, I yelled at myself for crippling a blessing I had worked so hard to get. In the end I was fortunate enough to wrestle with my habitual insecurities and squeak by.

So, after my ten-plus-year love affair with one of the most highly guarded aircraft ever designed, I was assigned to Beale Air Force Base, home of the coveted SR-71 Blackbird program as a midair refueler boom operator.

And, even though I had confirmed written orders, which I secretly carried like a passport, I still had a hard time accepting my luck. I felt that at any time, someone with authority would summon me to their office and snatch my papers away while barking, "Sorry, too bad. Not *you*. Wrong guy."

The very moment I completed flight school, rather than take time to celebrate with my graduating class, I jumped into my recently purchased used El Camino. It was already loaded to the gills with everything from a telephone to new sheets, pillows, and towels to every conceivable kitchen supply.

As I made my way north on the California highway, several deliveries were already being made to *my* apartment. I had everything planned to the absolute minute, so by the time I arrived, all of the major items, including a king-sized water bed, bureau, and oak wall units to proudly display my growing library, would be placed in their premeasured, assigned spots. With every passing mile my smile inside became wider and wider.

Part of the reason for my internal elation was that for the first time in my life, I *felt* clean. For once, my defensive, intensified brain was still. I didn't need to be afraid to death about the possibility of *some* possible thing that just might spring up and overtake me.

In the late hours of Friday afternoon, I eased my burdened Chevy into my assigned parking space. As exhausted as I was, I felt giddy like a wide-eyed preschooler on Christmas morning.

Once I stepped into my tiny one-bedroom apartment and closed the door, my eyes slowly addressed all the precious furniture that I had saved for by skipping meals for months on end. Out of excitement, I clapped my hands. I then whirled into a frenzy. I put together all the parts and cables to my stereo system so I could enjoy my music. Next, I washed and rewashed every kitchen item. In the bedroom, I carefully put on crisp new bedsheets. When everything was in its proper place, I celebrated by applying heavy layers of polish on every piece of wood. In my very own small world, it left a distinctive scent that reminded me of better days and how Mother would use the same wood polish that filled her home with the unique aroma. Strangely the connection made me feel happy. Maybe, my mind flashed, I was over Mother and all the consequences of my past.

Early the next evening, I finally emerged. I celebrated my new independence by grabbing a cheeseburger at a nearby Burger King. I then raced back so I could devour my prize in the privacy of my new home. Once done eating, which was my reward for all my hard work, I took inventory of all of my possessions—some that I'd had since my days in foster care. After taking it all in, my brain lurched. "Okay... now what?"

It was a startling new sensation. Since my days as Mother's prisoner, until just hours ago at my flight training, there had always been some gigantic hurdle for me to physically and mentally break through. Whether it be analyzing how to steal food from the bottom of garbage cans as a child, or standing in front of a mirror as a teenager, teaching myself how to properly pronounce the alphabet, or trying to master the in-flight refueling simulator, everything I did had become some inner, gut-wrenching quest.

For me, nothing came easily.

And now, I had a set of new flight suits in my closet, classical music that softly played from my stereo, and best of all, I, Dave Pelzer, could finally shut down that ever-spinning, fear-infested brain of mine and *safely* fall to sleep.

When I was a child, I constantly fidgeted on that worn army cot in the basement, terrified that Mother might materialize in the middle of the night like some venomous cobra, raising its hood a split second before striking me. In foster care and, for some reason, even more so in the air force, as much as I tried to just relax, a single sound in the night would cause my brain to snap into alert mode and I'd be up for the remainder of the evening. What no one knew was I would go for days without *any* sleep. Like some strung-out drug addict, I craved that intense feeling of being washed away in embracing, warm slumber.

Yet, after scanning the haven that I had created, I wasn't sure what to do next. I had always been on some quest, some type of mission to accomplish *something*. And now with a burger bomb in my full stomach and the peaceful stillness of my private dwelling, a new fear crept up my spine.

It was then that I realized I stayed busy simply by staying busy. Part of what drove me was the need to make up for all the time I lost while rotting away in the basement. Some of it stemmed from wanting to avoid the possibility of being made fun of or being rejected by others around me. But the biggest motivator was that I really didn't like myself all that much—how I looked, the sound of my voice, my lack of coordination, and my absence of common sense. So, I had concluded, the busier I stayed, the more I hunkered down, the more I tried to improve myself, that it might somehow elevate my standing, in my own eyes.

I leapt off the couch and went to clear my head by taking the first of many long walks. I strolled around the complex and far beyond. As I took in the new sights, I wondered what my own father must have thought of whenever he disappeared for a few moments after dinner when we were at the Russian River. Now as a young man beginning my own life's journey, I could not even begin to imagine the burdens that consumed him.

Suddenly I felt completely drained. It had been a very long day. As I returned to my apartment complex, I realized that it seemed like forever since I had first even dreamt of the possible goal of becoming an air crew member.

A short time later, as the sun's last rays pierced through my open window, I lay on my back on my bed. Outside children played at full speed, as if to try to capture every moment of their bright day while (I assumed) adults my age prepared to go out for the evening. With my right hand covering my eyes, I fell into a deep, tranquil sleep.

"Dave? Hey, David, have you heard anything I even said?" Patsy asked, snapping me out of my trance.

Looking down, I saw my finger was still tracing the outline of Stephen in the photo from long ago. "Sorry, I was just thinking 'bout some stuff."

"Dave, I really think that's part of your issues," Patsy stated sincerely, "sometimes… I just think you think *too* much."

As if Patsy had pulled on a private thread, I nodded into the phone. "Yeah, I know…" was all I could pull out from myself.

After my admission resonated, I realized that I had returned late last night from yet another extensive road trip and was exhausted. Out of fear of not having enough time, I had automatically jumped back into combat work mode.

"Patsy? I'm not trying to cut you off, but, I really think I *need* to get some sleep."

Not even a full minute later, safe in the private cocoon of my bedsheets, with only a small opening for me to breathe, my brain began to wind down. I could feel the euphoric sensation that I so craved as I drifted away. With my eyes fluttering closed, I smiled, thinking again of Stephen's joy-filled expression with the love of his mother's protective arms wrapped around him.

That evening, in my dream, I saw myself standing alone. I had a strong sense that I had been here before. I could clearly see the rays from the sun and the surrounding trees, but it was nothing like the Russian River. I turned completely around in a full circle, searching for something familiar, but nothing registered.

From behind me I picked up a faint noise. The gentle trickling sound came from a small stream. Suddenly everything clicked into place. When I blinked my eyes, my view sharpened. My heart began to race with excitement. I could not believe that out of all the thousands upon thousands of dreams of escape, that I had never dreamt of this before.

As I turned my head, I felt as if I were watching a film in slow motion. My peripheral vision seemed distorted, but in front of me, everything looked perfectly clear. Directly in front but just slightly above me I saw a small boy sitting on the end of a fallen log. The child's feet playfully dangled over the stream while his hands clutched a red-and-white plastic fishing pole. Studying the boy's face, I could see and even somehow feel his overwhelming joy that words could never describe.

His face was clean and his sparkling eyes were as wide as the sun. He showed no marks, slashes, burns, or even the slightest scratch. The boy's clothes were fresh and spotless. In a word, he was wholesome. As I stood in awe, I knew that at this precise moment the child felt nothing but absolute peace.

Even though I was just a few feet away, I knew the boy could not see me. As I studied the child's slightest movements, I began to feel light-headed. The more I scrutinized him, the weaker I became.

I broke from my stare. Just to be sure I was an adult, I looked down at my watch. I could clearly see the timepiece's unique dark blue face. But I also saw that there were no hands that displayed the time.

Feeling confused, I glanced back up. From behind the child, whom I guessed was between seven to eight years of age, I could see her. She too took my breath away. Her hair shone and her face glistened against the late morning sun. She too was happy and full of life. She straddled the log, with her hands protectively clinging to the back of the boy's belt.

I knew what was going to happen next. I felt a vibrating sensation fill every part of my body. *The* moment. That singular, simple fraction of a second that I had forever preserved in my heart like a piece of treasure, but which had also confused and haunted me for my entire life.

I was too afraid to blink or even breathe. After all this time, after all the crushing, isolating pain, I dared not miss it. I could feel the lower part of my throat constrict and an invisible band tighten around my chest. The boy leaned back against his mother's chest. He then closed his eyes. His mother, with one hand still clamped to his belt, drew her son closer, wrapping him in a loving embrace.

More than thirty years later and I could still reconnect to that feeling of my mother's moment of absolute pure love.

From just behind me, I heard footsteps as they pressed down on the small river rocks. Without turning, I knew it was Mother. Still overtaken by the moment that played out in front of me, I felt no fear.

"Was it real?" I asked without speaking.

Standing just beside me as if she too were looking up at our past, Mother flatly responded, "As real as it gets."

Startled, I turned my head toward Mother. Not because of her reply, but because I had heard my voice escaping from her mouth.

Fighting to regain a sense of calm, I simply asked out loud, "Why are you here?"

With a blink of her eyes, she stated, "You've summoned me."

"No," I denied. "Not here, never!"

For whatever amount of time passed, I deliberately said nothing. I simply flushed all thoughts away. I didn't want Mother burrowing inside my head.

Finally I caved. "Okay, what do you want?"

Suddenly, appearing right in front of me, she tilted her head. "What is it that you want?" Mother's tone changed my question into something completely different.

A heartbeat later, I felt completely drained. I looked back up. I could still see the fallen log but the boy and his mother were gone. For a moment, I felt as if my own brain teased me. But my heart knew different. It had happened.

Mother nodded in agreement.

Feeling as if I could barely stand, I looked down to see my right hand beginning to twitch. Gazing back up at the log, I knew what I craved, what I had always desired but had always eluded me. I let out a deep breath, as if ready to reveal my primal secret to both of us. I swallowed hard, feeling that this was the time and that this was indeed the place to unlock one of my primal lockboxes.

With my right hand stabilized, I reached out to my mother's hand. Just before the tips of my fingers grazed her skin, I glanced down to see her hand shake. She flashed me a sudden smile. The same one I had seen when she held me underwater, when she used both hands to choke me until I thought my eyes would suddenly pop from my head, and it told me that this was just another one of her games. A single thought screeched through my head: "Oh my God! Am I becoming her?"

The sound of Mother's nauseating laugh ricocheted inside my head as it awoke me from my dream.

CHAPTER 12

A BARGAIN MARRIAGE

IN THE VERY EARLY HOURS of the morning, while sitting in my private office at the house after paying a stack of bills, my tired eyes caught the special photo of Stephen and Patsy that was sitting on the side of my desk. And, as always, the captured moment made me smile.

I realized now with time and maturity that my relationship with Patsy was a push-pull contest of wills. Back then I never looked at myself and the extreme oddities that I brought into our marriage. I was too scared of everything. I just didn't see it.

Reflecting further, I thought maybe I simply didn't want to see it.

I had met Patsy while living at the same apartment complex by the Russian River after returning from one of my extensive walks. I had barely known her—just a few quick exchanges as I passed the pool area—when one late Friday evening, in a frantic state, Patsy sought protection at my apartment after she got into an argument with her boyfriend.

Within moments of closing the door behind me, Patsy's boyfriend, Greg, was pounding on my door, hurling threats against Patsy, then me. Greg's force was so intense I actually thought the hinges to the thick door might come off.

Patsy seemed so scared that she couldn't even cry. She leaned forward, cupping her hands to her face. "I'm so sorry. I know I shouldn't have come," she apologized.

My mind raced from Patsy's safety to Greg's battering to what my alarmed neighbors must be thinking to the likely arrival of the police with their blaring squad cars and flashing red lights. Yet all I could mutter to Patsy and myself was, "It's going to be fine. Trust me, *I* got this."

Thinking that Greg would surely burst through the door any second, I took Patsy by the hand and led her into my bedroom. Even though it was only a thin barrier, I closed the door behind me before returning to the front door. On the other side, Greg's slurred threats began to ebb. Finally, the pounding stopped.

I leaned toward the door. From the other side I could hear Greg's raspy breathing. Only after I heard Greg's heavy feet stumble down the staircase did I take a step back from the door. I then carefully made my way to the window to see if I could catch his fleeing shadow. Failing to do so, I focused on trying to listen. I calculated that Greg just might change his mind and reengage.

With nothing happening, I wasn't sure what to do. Only a few minutes before, after another long week of intensive flying, I had been safely asleep. Now, I couldn't even go into my bedroom, and suddenly my guard was up. So, I simply stood in a military parade rest stance with my legs slightly spread, back perfectly erect, and my hands clasped behind my back.

It was as if I were back in the basement, with my senses automatically snapping back to life. Back then, after so many years and countless terrifying situations, I became well-tuned to my darkened environment. I could sense Mother's mood by the weight of her walk whenever she shuffled from the living room to the kitchen to refill her drink.

And now I could decipher the gentle sounds of a woman laughing, while in the opposite direction I distinguished the blurred hues from someone's television.

After a fair amount of time, I needed to use the bathroom, which unfortunately for me was adjacent to the bedroom. And I needed something to put on. But being ever so anal, I always carefully folded and properly placed all my clothes in the closet that was (of course) next to my bathroom. And on top of all that had transpired I felt a little skittish about using the bathroom when I had a woman, whom I barely knew, in my bedroom.

I was oddly more concerned about startling Patsy than about being attacked by Greg. The last thing I wanted was for poor Patsy to think I might take advantage of the situation. So, as slowly and carefully as possible, I crept to the bedroom door. I tapped lightly a few times, straining for any response. When I didn't hear anything, I carefully opened it to discover that Patsy was fast asleep, snoring away.

Remembering when I was in the basement, walking on my tiptoes as I quietly made my way to the basin to steal water, I now carefully traipsed across the apartment's worn brown carpet, gently closing the bathroom door behind me. I then concentrated on trying to somehow pee as quietly as possible. Afterward, I stole a spare blanket from my closet to cover myself on the living room couch.

As much as my spent body wanted to escape with sleep, my whirling mind refused to let up. After more than an hour, I was still wide awake. As always, it was about feeling safe.

As a child, when Mother was done with me for the day, she would bellow from above that I was dismissed to sleep in the basement. In the dark, after scurrying to put together a clunky World War II green army cot for my bed, I would not allow myself to fall asleep until after I heard *her* make the journey from the living room to the bathroom, and, finally, to her squeaky bed. Just to be sure, it wasn't until after I heard Mother's distinctive snore that I felt safe enough to allow my brain to switch off.

So now, still lying on my back and unable to capture any rest, I wasn't all that frustrated. I wasn't even overly upset. It simply was what it was. As much as I craved to escape to my world of dreams, at the end of the day I had been there for a girl in need. As I stared at the ceiling and kept my internal radar focused on my surroundings, I liked how the new sensation made me feel.

The next morning, after giving Patsy a glass of OJ, she spilled over with apologies. "Sorry 'bout last night. Greg's not really my boyfriend, not anymore. He doesn't even have a job. He thinks, just 'cause, sometimes, we go out… that he thinks he owns me."

Smacking both hands on her hips, Patsy suddenly changed her tone and announced, "Ain't no one, and I mean no one, *owns* me! Not now, not ever. I do what I want, when I want. And that's that."

I wasn't taken aback. I instantly knew that Patsy was making her statement more to herself than to me. But unlike me, Patsy actually had the guts to state her beliefs, while I wimpishly hid behind so many impregnable layers. As Patsy stood in front of me, I became captivated by her deep inner strength. I could never step up and speak out about how I wished to be treated, let alone ask for the respect that, at times, I so selfishly craved.

"Anyhow," Patsy went on, "we got into it 'cause Greg thinks I got a thing for you."

I nearly spat out my orange juice on Patsy's blouse. "That doesn't make any sense, why would he think that?"

With her hand on the knob to the front door, Patsy stopped midstride, leaned in, and kissed me on the cheek. "'Cause I do." I could feel the warmth of her breath on the side of my face.

A sudden rush filled me. I couldn't believe it. The party girl of the complex, who could be with any guy she desired, liked *me*? Before Patsy could make her way down the outside stairs, I threw away my protective shield.

"Hey," my nervous voiced quavered, "I gotta go to the Bay Area. Would you…?"

Without hesitation Patsy gave me a nod. "Love to. Just give me a few minutes. Come on, take me home."

As I walked with Patsy, we happily chatted away, but I had no idea of what either one of us said. My head was swimming. I couldn't stop smiling. Above me, there wasn't a cloud in the sky. The jasmine plants gave off a thick, sweet fragrance. I knew it was going to be an absolutely beautiful, perfect day.

As Patsy and I approached her mother's apartment, our hands brushed together. I began to take her hand when we came upon the rumpled figure of Greg. Before he could blurt out any of his rehearsed threats, Patsy quickly disappeared into the apartment.

I looked down at his clenched hands, then back up at his strained face. I could tell by his unkempt hair, wrinkled clothes, and body odor that poor Greg had probably been up all night watching Patsy's apartment while sitting in his rusted-out late-'70s silver Honda.

"Hey four eyes, get this, Patsy, she's mine. Understand?" Greg stated as he took a full step toward me.

I had little concern. After the countless beatings from Mother, as well as being pummeled relentlessly by the junior high school bully while in foster care, I had racked up enough broken glasses to know when I was about to be attacked. I also knew a blow-hard when I saw one. I had seen *his* kind a million times before. And now part of me was fed up by the charade.

"Hey, are you even listening to me? I'm talkin' to you!" Greg bellowed.

I nodded to myself. *Yeah, I hear you.*

"I tell you what. I got a thirteen-degree black belt. I can so kick your ass. Right here, right now," he amplified while shaking his head and almost biting his lip.

In order to not set him off, I remained silent. I studied Greg's body language to see if he would either lean against one hip or begin to pull his arm back. From experience, I knew that would be the signal, giving me a full second to defend myself before Greg could strike.

Yet the more Greg blathered, just as Mother had done her best to run me down, the more I wanted to vomit out all the crud that I had swallowed for so many years. In my head, I wanted to decry: "*You're* pathetic. Absolutely, completely pa-the-tic! You're a wimp of the worst kind. You're worse than white trash. Black belt my ass, you don't even have one to hold up your stained Levi's.

"Look at yourself. Why would anyone be with the likes of you? For God's sake, take a shower, brush your *tooth*, get a haircut and put on some clean clothes. Come on, get a job. Get a life.

"Hell, you live with your momma and when you're with Patsy, she tells me that she makes you sleep on the floor."

But outwardly, I maintained my hardwired passive stance in front of Mr. Kung Fool.

In my fantasy-fueled mind, I even went so far as to visualize that if needed, I could bring Greg down in two, maybe three moves. It would all be over in less than a couple of seconds.

However, a full, clear breath later, as much as I wanted for *once* to push back, I knew *I* could never do that. I could never afford to become like Mother.

If I received one gift from Mother and all that transpired between us, it was that she in fact made me "want it" more, to dig from deep within to become a better person. After years of pain and loss as a child, in the end I was lucky enough to be able to appreciate the everyday gifts around me.

Even when Mother was at her worst against me, I came to the conclusion that Mother was horribly consumed by her own misery. And now, as this wretch of a young person yammered white noise, I felt that Greg too would most likely live out his days with little to no sense of worth and never savor the basic joys of everyday life.

With just a glance at Greg, I could tell that he had endured a hard life. Which was why he acted the way he did. I knew it, as did he. And, without stating the obvious, Greg certainly must have known that I could see through his facade.

So as not to provoke, as always, I remained feeble and even overly submissive. As taught as a child, I knew how to play that role—chin down, and with my shoulders slumped forward. And even though part of my ego wanted me to erupt, I swallowed it.

I gave my antagonist a slight nod. To me it signaled my strength to withdraw. But I also knew that Greg would take it as a signal of his superiority.

I took a full step back before turning and walking away. As I did, I listened for Greg trying to rush me. But all I could hear was him yelling for all the world to hear, "Yeah, I thought so. Next time, you watch out."

And just as I had when Mother used to screech at me, just inches away from my face, with her saliva covering me, I shut it down. Back then, I was indeed scared to death, for I knew she could lose it and in a heartbeat snap my neck. Yet I would barely hear or feel anything, as if there were some thick wall of water between us.

For me it became a matter of conditioning.

The rest of the day was magical. Patsy and I chatted nonstop the entire way to the Bay Area, where we visited my foster parents. On the drive back to Yuba City, I cracked the door slightly, revealing, in part, why I had been placed in foster care. Patsy then opened up on some elements from her past. As she did, suddenly everything made sense—why she hung out with such a rowdy group, partied as much as she did, even why she settled with someone like Greg. As Patsy carefully spoke about her relationship with her parents and her siblings, I felt that she too carried a deep desire for approval from those who had hurt her the most. While part of me felt sorry for Patsy, I was more impressed by how strong she seemed. Outwardly, I knew, she was much stronger than I.

It was then that I realized that *because* of our similar past, *and* our unique connection, we might actually be *good* for each other. I knew that Patsy liked me. My main hope was that she realized I was definitely a better person than Greg.

I began to compute that after being with all those *Gregs*, Patsy would see me and appreciate me all the more! As a current of thoughts swam around my head, I smiled at myself. Man, *I* got this all figured out!

After getting off the interstate, Patsy's mood slowly changed. I didn't notice at first. The whole day was such a one-of-a-kind experience for me. But looking over at

Patsy, I could clearly see how withdrawn she had become. I felt her pain.

With my defensive radar switched back on, I picked up on Patsy's slumped posture and how tightly she kept clenching her hands. Under her breath, she muttered, "I don't want to go home."

I knew exactly how Patsy felt. Of the many things that Mother conditioned me to do, one was to run home at full speed the moment school let out. For the first few years, I did exactly as commanded, trying to impress Mother with my timid loyalty. But as I matured, and as Mother became even more demented, sometimes I would deliberately slow my pace. It helped me with my shut-down process—going from looking up at the boundless, blue-streaked skies, to how I could possibly counter her attacks.

"I'm just tired. Tired of everything," Patsy almost cried. "I don't know if he's gonna be there. And, I don't want to get the other end of it from my mom. I don't need this shit."

I reached over to hold her hand. In that moment, I swallowed hard before straining, "I don't want you to take this the wrong way, but, if you want… you can stay at my place."

Patsy's eyes lit up and she flashed me a wide smile. "Love to."

From that moment on, unless I was at the base, Patsy and I became inseparable. It was all so new and exciting, to the point of intoxicating. Not only was Patsy my first true friend who was a girl, but my first official girlfriend.

But after returning from my first overseas deployment, in which I was away for a month, I discovered that Patsy, after getting into a series of arguments with her mother, had moved into my apartment. At first I felt violated. A second later, shock took over. As much time as we had spent together, I still felt the apartment was *my* place, my sanctuary. Even as the thoughts flushed through me, I knew I was being immature and selfish.

After I swallowed a huge lump in my throat, Patsy calmed me down. "Come on. It's not like I'm not over here all the time."

Taking a psychological step back, I knew that Patsy and her mother clashed quite a bit and that Patsy hated sleeping on the ancient living room couch while her unemployed brother shared the second bedroom with his girlfriend. And because Patsy was also between jobs, she helped her ailing mother by cooking all the meals for her *and* the herd of family members that constantly came and went at all hours of the day, which forced Patsy to do even more work cleaning up the entire place after the notorious food raids.

"I'm sick an' tired of being everyone's slave. And not once does anyone say 'thank you.' It's like it's expected of me. It's always been like that," Patsy fumed.

I knew how Patsy felt. Toward the end, before I was taken away, even my own brothers, Ron and Stan who were once my saviors, and especially Russell, whom I had dubbed Mother's Little Nazi, seemed to turn against me. They seemed to take pleasure in the fact that while they played, watched TV, and were fed like royalty, I was the *thing* who cleaned up after every meal (which I was not allowed to eat), scoured the bathroom twice a day, and had to use my fingers to clean out the soiled cat box.

"Okay," I simply said. "All right."

For the first few months, everything seemed carefree. And even though I was way out of my comfort zone on so many levels, feeling that everything in my personal life was going way too fast, Patsy more than proved her merit. Once when I became so sick that I couldn't even get out of bed, Patsy took care of me. When I discovered my beloved foster father, Mr. Turnbough, had cancer, Patsy made nearly every lengthy visit with me and was by my side the afternoon Harold passed away.

Whenever tensions arose, before I could spool up and imagine the worst, Patsy would let me vent before reassuring me that things between us would get better.

Yet I began to feel, due to my own insecurities, that even though Patsy and I shared a great deal, we were simply two different types of people. In part because of my travels around the globe, I liked to stay home and relax by reading and listening to music, while Patsy, understandably, enjoyed going out with her group of unruly friends. While I was advancing my air force career, Patsy seemed content not looking for employment. Whenever she did land a job, it was only for a short time, and somehow, for some odd string of reasons, Patsy was always the victim of never being paid. On the surface, we seemed fine. But after the initial thrill of someone new in my life, internal cracks began to develop.

For example, since joining the air force, I had always been proud to save two hundred dollars a month, but with Patsy I was no longer able to do so and was even quietly dipping into my protective savings. It was in no way Patsy's fault. The decision was *completely* my own. For the most part, it was small things—money for day trips, movies, some nice dinners, and a few bucks for Patsy to have as walking around money. But after a while, when I would literally empty my wallet to give Patsy some money for the day, which meant I would have to skip another lunch at the base, the silent seed of resentment began to take root.

One morning when I was walking out the door for work, Patsy, who had been acting odd, suddenly burst into tears, confessing she needed "a few hundred" to cover a *small* traffic violation or she faced the possibility of jail. With my internal clock ticking away, computing how much time I was losing as I stood on the outside landing, my astounded brain slipped into the wrong gear.

My overzealous mouth zipped off, "My God! How long have you known about this?"

It seemed to take forever for Patsy to finally admit, "A long time ago. It doesn't matter. I'm telling you now." Patsy continued to cry. "I just didn't want to upset you. The whole thing happened *way* before I met you. It's not even really my fault. Again, it's not important!"

My ears picked up on a pattern, a mantra of sorts—it's not important, I worry too much, she didn't want to make me mad. It seemed to me that seconds before some "problem bomb" would detonate, Patsy would suddenly inform me of some unexpected, impending device.

Thinking of my crew already mission planning our next flight without me and how my aircraft commander was a stickler for one being on time, I nervously checked my Seiko watch. I shook my head.

"I'm sorry, really I am. I don't even have enough in my checking…"

"Your card," Patsy broke in. "It's okay. I checked into it. *You* can go over to the courthouse and give 'em your credit card. It's fine, really, it's no big deal."

I fled without helping out. I drove my El Camino well over the speed limit, arriving just as my aircraft commander mockingly said they were about to deploy a search party.

Throughout the day, I was so consumed with Patsy that my copilot finally leaned over and pointed out several mistakes on the critical weight and balance form that was my responsibility. As I took out my slide rule for the umpteenth time, Lt. Averett whispered to me. "Jafbo, this ain't like you. Come on, clear the mechanism."

As much as I wanted to, I couldn't get myself to flip off the Patsy switch.

At the end of the day, I sped back home, ran up the stairs, and almost crashed through my door. With my keys still in the door, I shouted out for Patsy. When I heard and found nothing, I flew back down the stars and sprinted over to her mother's place. I banged on the door and entered without waiting for permission.

With my hands on my hips, I struggled to catch my breath, when, to the left of me, I made out the image of Patsy, sitting comfortably on the couch, seemingly without a care in the world. Patsy turned away from her TV show and stated, "Told you. You worry too much. Got the money from Mom. See, no problem."

As thankful as I was, I was beyond stunned. I wasn't sure what to think. After a few minutes, I slowly walked alone back to my apartment, feeling the sudden need to take a shower.

It seemed like not so long ago that I hadn't wanted to be alone, and now I felt scared and closed in. I knew it was my ego. I knew it was wrong. But yet, I felt I deserved to be with someone different. But, I also believed that no one else would even look at me.

So, I did as I had taught myself years ago—I kept my hesitations deeply buried, thinking, hoping, and even praying that somehow *Patsy* would change so that we would not only become a better, stronger couple, but live happily ever after.

At times situations seemed to reach a tipping point, and I wanted to throw up my hands and shout out, "That's it. I can't do this anymore. I'm sorry, but it's over!" But then I would suddenly be deployed to Japan, England, or other parts of the globe, for weeks or months at a time.

Halfway around the world, I felt relieved not to worry about Patsy, or the swirl of her family drama that never seemed to cease. But weeks passed, and when I would call her from overseas, Patsy would excitedly exclaim how much weight she had suddenly lost, or how she had finally landed a fantastic job, or, most importantly of all, how much *she* wanted to make things better. Then, I truly missed her.

At night, I'd lie on my bed replaying all the good times Patsy and I had shared. And even though I had heard wild rumors about Patsy from scores of people, it somehow made me feel all the more special because she chose to be with me rather than anybody else. In some odd sense, it also made me long for Patsy all the more.

When I returned from overseas with a few days off, it was like a honeymoon. Alone together, everything seemed so peaceful and calm. But after three, maybe four days, small little digs would creep up. Even though there was so much tension between Patsy and her mother, Patsy couldn't stay away from her. So to offer support, I'd visit with Patsy's mom and other overly loud family members who also happened to drop by. And it seemed the moment I returned home, Patsy would always, somehow, just have lost her job, and again with no compensation.

My honed instincts knew what was actually happening around me. I just couldn't (or more so, didn't want to) accept that after all Patsy and I had shared—Patsy might be fibbing to me.

One evening after much prodding, Patsy convinced me to join her at her favorite bar, the Silver Dollar Saloon. Even before walking in together, I became tense. I stood out as the only person without boots, a gigantic belt buckle, a hat, and a toothpick rolling around in my mouth. To seal my fate, I couldn't dance, which Patsy loved to do. After a couple of hours and nursing two beers, I stood alone at the end of the stale-smelling bar, watching Patsy dance endlessly with her old friends. She only seemed to come over when she wanted another refreshment before scurrying back to dance. I knew Patsy was simply having fun, but feeling uncomfortable, alone, and now with a pounding headache, I felt that I had endured enough.

Back home, Patsy and I got into our first major argument. I wanted her to know how *I* had sacrificed for her and how thankful *she* should be! Patsy tried to tell me how she felt cooped up and just wanted to have some fun. To me it seemed an easy fix. If I could only get Patsy to understand how I was out of my safety box, while at the same time swallowing my pride by trying *not* to be overly judgmental, she would appreciate me all the more! Easy.

Yet I felt I couldn't get a full sentence out, which made me start from the beginning, again and again. After a few minutes, with rising voices, I realized how badly I was swimming after her.

Then I tripped one of Patsy's circuit breakers. Her frustrated face suddenly turned dark crimson. "You are not my father! You don't own me. You don't tell me what to do. Ever!"

From my stance at the far end of the kitchen, in order to calm her down with an immediate submission of apology, I took a step toward Patsy, knowing this whole thing had gone too far. I didn't even process the true meaning of the feelings behind her words. My sole intention was to immediately end the confrontation.

But, things escalated to the point that I stayed up all night sitting on the kitchen floor with my back against the wall, shivering and thinking, "Oh my God! What just happened?"

Then after returning home from the Bay Area, where I fled to seek solace from all the drama that weekend, I knew I had to end it. Alone in my apartment, I kept the stereo off but turned on all the lights as I carefully packed Patsy's things and gently placed them beside the door.

Later that Sunday evening when Patsy came over, I didn't even get out a single sentence of what I had planned to say. I couldn't (or wouldn't) pull the trigger. We talked, we yelled, and then we cried, before creating the perfect quick fix, a plan so we could try to try again.

All in all, we tried again, and again, and again.

Our cycling continued until Patsy became pregnant. After a roller coaster of emotions, Patsy and I concluded that because of what we had already endured, that a baby could somehow make things better—make us better.

In every aspect, our son, Stephen, was beyond a blessing. As a small boy, he was the happiest child on the planet. From sunup until he collapsed from pure exhaustion, Stephen played and laughed. And, like all children, Stephen gave Patsy and me something we'd never had in our own childhoods: unconditional love.

But, eight years later, the strain became too much. In the end, it was Patsy who had the guts to pull the trigger on our marriage.

By then I had retired from the air force and begun a new job that required I travel, often for weeks at a time. While I was on the road, Patsy was kind enough to find me a small place in Guerneville, while she eventually settled for a country home just down the dirt road from her mother's trailer, in the same town where Patsy was raised and had longed to live.

Thirty days after our divorce was final, I sat in the back row when Patsy, dressed in a cowgirl outfit and boots, strolled down the aisle to marry her cowboy—a man fifteen years her junior, whom to my knowledge never rode a horse or worked on a ranch.

After the ceremony, Patsy and I embraced. Then with all my heart I wished her the happiness that she deserved.

And now, more than ten years later, with another broken relationship under *my* belt, I *felt* it. A small, almost electrical jolt-like sensation. "Oh my God!" I stated to no one. "*I* am such an ass."

In the last few months, ever so slowly, intentionally or not, I had begun to peel back some of the hardened layers of my life and examine how they might have affected my time with Marsha, yet I had given little thought to my marriage with Patsy.

When Patsy and I married, we both worked to settle any differences and prepare for our child's arrival, which included moving on base. We decided that Patsy would be a stay-at-home mom, while I vowed to myself that I would do everything possible to provide for my family.

Like my father before me, I brought home the paycheck, and with my first lawn mower, I would cut and edge the grass once a week and water it every day for half an hour. I even proudly washed the family car at a precise time every Saturday morning, before the temperature got too high.

By the time Stephen arrived, his room was already crammed with a safari of stuffed animals. When he was two, in the early morning hours before I left for work, I'd happily lay out his long yellow Slip 'N Slide, connect yet another one just behind it, fill his plastic play pool, and set out his army of toys for the day. In the late afternoon, when I returned home, Stephen and I played until Patsy called us in for dinner. Then at the end of his day, Stephen usually collapsed on my chest after I'd read from his favorite book, *Are You My Mother?*, which I would read while imitating various voices.

Yet far beneath the layers of being the ecstatic father to such a beautiful child, as Stephen grew, I began to realize how linearly focused I had become on providing for my family, while I gave little consideration to being a good husband to Patsy.

On my air force enlisted income, Patsy and I did everything possible to make *every* penny count. Whenever we shopped at the base grocery store, I'd whip out my little calculator, adding every item so Patsy and I could abide by our budget. If it looked like we might go over by even a mere dollar, I'd stop the process and return any item I suddenly deemed unnecessary. And while I was quite proud to have all household items paid for and even provide Patsy with a meager allowance, it never seemed to be enough. At times, only after digging into my vacant billfold for the umpteenth time, I'd explode over whatever purchase I believed was so imperative at that particular moment.

Besides deep feelings of inadequacy, old tendencies of servitude began to creep in. I was proud that I was responsible for my wife and blessed young boy, but there always seemed to be *some* never-yielding situation regarding either overspending of funds that I didn't have, or some form of unnecessary family drama. Whenever I seemed to have some rare time off, Patsy and I would suddenly be summoned by one of her siblings to make the hour-plus drive that had something to do with Patsy's mother. After putting in all that I did with the air force, I simply wanted to chill out, without any interference, so I could be with *my* family.

Over time the finances became a major issue. But it wasn't about the money as much as it was about trust and all the distress that came with me mopping up the aftermath. After a string of checks bounced at the base's stores, I was ordered to my first sergeant's office, where I stood in front of his desk while being dressed down on my financial responsibilities. More than once it was mentioned that I might lose my security clearance, which meant I would be taken off flight status.*

In my own black-and-white world, when it came to money I was never behind—ever. Before I was married it had all been so simple—do without for now in order to save all the more for the future.

I did all that I could, explaining, pleading, and then, wrongly, even lashing out at Patsy, all the time trying to get her to *understand* the consequences of the situation. Yet, before the next pay period, especially when I was overseas, *something* would suddenly arise—unforeseen problems with the car, a broken washing machine, or some other unexpected expense that drained our funds. We might only be short fifty dollars, but to me it was as if we were behind by thousands. For me, it was a matter of pride.

I was so ashamed.

I felt like I couldn't catch up, and from deep within it killed me. Even years later, before Stephen turned four, when I landed a part-time job in juvenile hall and I

* At the time some of the members of our squadron, including myself, were secretly involved with the highly classified F-117 Stealth Fighter program.

stashed away the mighty sum of a thousand dollars, I still felt that at any moment Patsy's spending might topple us over into the financial abyss.

Ever since I'd pledged the words "I do," ever so slowly, I had begun to feel the same type of intense fear I had when I was in the basement, where I applied my mind like an abacus, calculating every move for the mere chance at scrounging food. I didn't pay any attention to my induced agitation until one morning when I unintentionally saw Patsy getting dressed, and I could clearly see the holes in her undergarments. Later that day, while on a rare trip to a high-end shopping mall in Sacramento, as Patsy chatted to a makeup lady who informed Patsy that if she made a single purchase, Patsy would receive sixty-four dollars of free items, I immediately shut her down. "Nope. Can't afford it. Come on, let's go. Next time, next time."

Years later, sitting alone in my elaborately decorated office, those cold-hearted, explosive words rattled me to my core. I could only imagine how Patsy must have felt.

Even back then I knew I was being too hypercritical. And, I was too judgmental of Patsy. For all my principles, as much as I fought to be a good man and a helpful person, I realized I could have been, *should* have been, a far better husband.

Patsy deserved better.

CHAPTER 13

TENTACLE

OF MY MANY ISSUES, my need to fix everything, prove my worth, and to please others no matter the toll, had always been a dominant part of my being. And at times, even when I knew I was hurtling into some black hole, I refused to let go or alter my course because of my ironclad belief that things had to, somehow, get better.

During one of my many midnight strolls, I realized part of my justification for clinging to Marsha was because it was my second marriage, and I desperately wanted to make it work and to somehow make *her* life perfect. I had felt if I could give more to Marsha than I had given to Patsy, including anything that Marsha craved, in the end, everything would work itself out.

I met Marsha a full year after my divorce from Patsy, and after moving to Guerneville, where I lived like a hermit. Internally, I was broken and lonely. In twelve months' time I had already endured so much.

First I learned that *escaping* to Guerneville was nothing more than some linear obsession. Somehow, without ever wanting to admit it, I had always used the Russian

River as the singular attachment to the happier times of my lost childhood.

Living there as an adult, I experienced the grungy lifestyle of the mostly unemployed residents who barely sustained themselves through a complex system of either bartering or trying to pawn off "used-used" stuff. At first, I didn't pay all that much attention. As the norm, I simply overlooked the immensity of the situation in order to justify my lifelong desire.

During my time at the Russian River, and after a string of poor choices, I broke away from a speaking firm after I discovered that my first two books, which were claimed to have been *published*, were simply *printed*. And then I became horrified when I discovered that the person who managed my affairs and fought with me tooth and nail whenever I dared to ask a mere question, was not only a toxic, pathological manipulator, but had systematically embezzled the company's funds.

In the refrigerator-like setting of my moldy Guerneville studio home, I had truly sensed something was off with some of the members of the speaking firm. Because of my minimal self-esteem, rarely did I summon the guts to try to resolve the deteriorating situations that were created by this individual. Instead, I focused on my strong desire to prove myself by righting any other impossible calamity, and *then* I could receive whatever I deserved at a later date.

I fought to fix my latest complication by starting my own business and finding a *real* publisher. As thrilled as I was, before I even signed the one-sided contract with a small publisher (which I signed in part because I felt soiled from my experience with the speaking firm and had the intense fear that no one would touch me), I immediately knew elements were, once again, way off.

But Marsha was my saving grace. She had recently been hired by the publisher, and my first book was her initial project as an new editor. She had a soft voice and a gentle nature. Compared to others from the speaking firm, who were arrogant and full of bluster, Marsha was a breath of fresh air. But because a series of mistakes made by the publisher—contracts had been forgotten to be mailed, which affected deadlines for the next seasonal releases—and because my book was viewed as a filler, *A Child Called "It"* was allotted very little production time.

However, because I had been disgusted with the *editing* of the previous *printed* version, I pleaded with my new editor for more time to make the book better. So, what began with a few minutes on the phone once a day to gloss over a scene soon became six-hour discussions late at night with me breaking down the most minute parts of every sentence. One night, after calling it quits at three a.m., I realized just how lonely I had become. Besides driving three hours one way to see my son, my only form of human contact was standing in line to pick up my mail at the local post office.

Marsha had become a lifeline of sorts.

Even though I was intrigued by Marsha, the anal, protective side of me knew how foolishly I was beginning to think. But after another late-night round of editing during which Marsha and I discussed our spiritual beliefs, I suddenly lowered my guard. It was when her soft voice adamantly told me that God not only loved me, but more importantly, that I should not be so ashamed of my past, that I began to have feelings for her.

Another part of the attraction was that I felt we were a team. I became elated that, for once, I didn't feel like I was being used and that I could finally trust someone wholeheartedly.

When the extensive new edits seemed to garner little attention, Marsha and I developed an us-against-them, back-to-back mentality. As a team, our first real challenge came after Marsha called me in a frantic state after a marketing meeting.

"Dave, I just came out… and I can't believe it. I just can't."

With my brain fighting to understand my editor's message, I pleaded, "Okay, take a deep breath. What's wrong?"

"Someone on the staff said—"

Exhaling with relief, I jumped in. "Marsha, it's okay. I know all about the whole *The Child Called "Shit"* thing. It's no big deal."

"No!" Marsha cried out. "You don't get it. Someone said your books are all fake! This person said that…"

I know Marsha kept talking, but my brain failed to register anything after the word fake.

"So, we were all in the meeting going over different titles coming out, and anyway, when it came to your book, Rochelle, whom you know from PR, well, she stood up and practically yells, 'I don't know Dave Pelzer, I've never read a word of his books, but I *know* he's a liar!'"

For a few seconds I barely had the strength to hold the phone. Of all things, in a million years I never would have…

"Dave, I don't know what to do. I'm in a tight spot."

My first thought was, "Okay, hang on, *I* can fix this. I can talk to Rochelle, I could speak to the president of the publishing company... I could come up with a list of all my foster parents, my teachers, anybody who knew me, I can do it! This is so doable!"

"David, everybody knows that I spent all that time with your book. And some may think that I'm in on this."

Overwhelmed with shame, I instantly confessed, "I swear to God Almighty, it's not a lie. It's not! Hold it, hold on." My mind rapidly switched gears, "Mr. Ziegler, my fifth grade teacher who pushed for me to get rescued, he's in the book. He wrote a perspective. Didn't you talk to him?"

"My God." Marsha admitted, "I forgot. I spoke to him, and to Mrs. Konstan, your fourth grade teacher; Mrs. Woodworth, your English teacher; and your foster mother, Mrs. Turnbough; and even her daughter, Mary, and son in-law, Del. They all told me everything."

I shook my head, feeling relieved. "All right, great. Problem solved." Then a full second later, my brain suddenly changed to another track. "Marsha, wait a sec. Do me a favor... back up. Give me your statement again."

As Marsha replayed the scene, I wrote down what Rochelle had proclaimed.

When she finished I proudly stated, "How can any person take seriously, let alone believe, someone whose statement begins with 'I don't *know* so and so, and I've *never* read his books'? Come on!"

Marsha sighed. "I kinda thought that too, but it was like no one even caught *that*, like it didn't matter. It was like everyone only heard what they wanted to hear. So when she said that, all at once, everyone turned and looked at me as if I had something…"

Instantly, I reconnected to an old familiar feeling of my private virus once again spreading onto others.

I fought to make Marsha feel better. "I'm sorry. So sorry. I never would have thought anything like this…" I couldn't even finish my pathetic apology. I had simply run out of words.

For the next several days I tried to reach the president of the publishing company, and just like before, when I'd had to chase him for the forgotten contracts, for some reason he was always unavailable and failed to return a single call.

I then learned that the staff's initial excitement about the book had suddenly evaporated after Rochelle's proclamation. Then, after another string of errors when the book was released, it was only available in a few stores. Soon afterward I phoned my editor to apologize that after all the genuine enthusiasm and all the hours breaking down every word to its core, I felt terrible that I'd wasted so much of Marsha's time. As we spoke about the obvious failure of the book, we both joked about how dysfunctional a publisher specializing in self-improvement seemed. As crushed and embarrassed as I was, after hanging up the phone, I was extremely thankful that I had someone on my side.

Later that fall, after having met Marsha and spending the hundreds of hours on the phone, and as she began to recognize her growing dismay over the antics at the publishing house, I abruptly offered her a position as my director if she wanted to leave Florida. But the very moment I hung up the phone, I thought, "Oh my God, what in the hell did you just do?"

I knew how stupidly impulsive and desperate I was being, but part of me was fed up with feeling defeated and alone. I felt that no matter how hard I worked and for all my qualities as a person, even the Guerneville grunge looked down on me. The only person besides my son that wanted anything to do with me lived over three thousand miles away.

The selfish part of me felt that with the demise of the book, I might lose my connection with Marsha. And after all of our time together, mainly on the phone, I didn't want to revert to my hermit ways.

I fully realized that Marsha was more than eight years my junior and that she had grown up sheltered by her overly protective, religious parents and had never journeyed beyond the state's lines. But as with all things, I believed that no matter the obstacles, *I* could make it all work out.

Stopping myself as I reached the top of another hill during my extended walk, I shook my head at my conundrum. For a plethora of reasons, as a couple, Marsha and I had never had a chance. Besides both of us coming from two different worlds, there was always the roller coaster drama that never ended. There was always something to contend with.

After being on the road for weeks, I flew into Florida in order to drive Marsha practically nonstop across the country to her new setting in Guerneville. When we arrived at the Russian River we were met with a monsoon-like flood. And that was after we were still licking our wounds from our first fight, which became so heated that we both questioned the logic of our decision.

Then there was Stephen, whom I felt I couldn't see enough of. There were instances when I would only be home for a mere few hours taking care of paperwork, laundry, and prepping for my next tour before racing off to be with my son. As the pattern continued, I felt that by being with Stephen, I was abandoning Marsha. At times, I found myself pleading for Marsha's patience and approval. I constantly scrambled to somehow make things right. But I always felt that no matter what I did, or how much I bargained, I came up short.

Then whenever Marsha and I planned to have a moment for only ourselves to escape to a rare movie matinee or inexpensive dinner, *something* always happened.

Part of our frustration came from Patsy. Even though she was remarried by then, she was always extremely behind with her rent and all of their bills. Whenever she called she seemed panic-stricken, claiming that if I didn't help out at that very moment, our son would obviously be adversely affected. I always erred on the side of caution, not wanting to take that chance. And because Patsy had no bank accounts and never-ending credit issues, I spent most of my off time, which should have been dedicated to Marsha, on the phone for hours at a time tracking down different agencies. I would then run to the bank to obtain money orders before driving twenty-plus miles away to the nearest UPS store so I could spend my limited funds on numerous overnight packages.

After the third incident, Marsha became livid. She had every right to be. "She is using you! She and her *cowboy* husband are just sitting outside on their white plastic chairs, sucking on the last drops from last weekend's kegger.

"I know why you're doing this. As much as you think it's about Stephen, part of you is still trying to prove yourself to her. Like she's gonna appreciate you?

"Sometimes you can be so stupid! I can't believe you don't see that Patsy always calls once a month, just like clockwork. You think that by being so nice, that by giving everything you have, that everyone's going to like you? Do you even know how many people laughed at you behind your back because of the publishing contract that you signed? They know, it went all around. They got the Outstanding Young Person of the World for five points *below* what they pay to a nobody! And you have to sell a half a million copies before you even get that. What were you thinking?

"Or what about the conversations I had with Kerry at the PR department before I came out to California? You thought that by being goody-goody polite, that Kerry would do even the minimum for you. She thinks you're weak. That's why she shuts you out whenever you even question her on her BS! She doesn't care. All anyone cares about is what they can get from you. That's it.

"Look at all the volunteer work you've done. When this or that group tells you how hard up they are, convincing you to do three, four, five events in a single day for free, *and* you pay for all the expenses! Then, the next time around, suddenly they have more than enough funds to pay someone else, full ride, for a few minutes of presentation. And they cuss me out when I feel I have to beg just for expenses. Why? Because they somehow think you shouldn't get a dime, because Dave Pelzer with all his awards, because he was rescued from his psycho mother from hell, *still* owes everyone! Huh, bet you didn't know about that, did you?"

Suddenly switching back to Patsy, Marsha continued, "And Lord knows how many times Patsy calls you that I don't know about when you're on the road. Is there some reason that you won't tell me why you seem to spend more time driving to be with your son than with me?"

I didn't want to tell Marsha that, in part because Stephen's mother had a string of boyfriends before she remarried, whenever the three of us were together, Stephen seemed distant to Marsha. So, I thought, in order to avoid any additional conflict between Stephen and Marsha, at times I would pack my bags and venture off to spend the weekend alone with my son.

In the beginning, I fought to keep my mouth shut and my feelings buried, just as I had with Patsy. After a while, I'd carefully *tried* to present my side to Marsha. Yet I could not get her to understand that because of Stephen, I *had* to assist whenever Patsy called. I couldn't take the chance of exposing Stephen to yet another unfortunate outcome. My need to protect my son made me an emotional hostage.

As the incidents with Patsy continued, followed by Marsha's increasingly lengthy outbursts, I began to feel I was damned. I was getting it from both ends. *I* was tired, *I* was fed up and I felt *I* was the one trying to do everything, be everything, for everyone.

Once, when Marsha seemed more upset than usual about Patsy and after what seemed like forever of her ridiculing me over and over, my insides began to shake. I felt as if I were going to throw up or have to flee to the bathroom to relieve myself. I spun around and started to walk away from Marsha to get some space.

Fighting to clear my head while trying not to reveal my internal demon, I turned back to Marsha and stated, "I do what I have to do because he's my son…" Letting my less than feeble confession hang in the air, I followed up with more of an analytical retort. "You think for a second that I don't know? Really? For God's sake, I can't afford to take the chance. I've already put him through enough."

"Enough of what?" Marsha lobbed back.

I asked, "Remember after their town flooded and they lost their house and had to live in a motel?"

"I remember you draining money from your checkbook to hand over to Patsy, yes."

"You should have seen the look in Stephen's eyes. He lost everything—the toys he'd had since he was a baby, all his clothes, *everything*. It's like, since the divorce and the flood, Stephen's lost his childhood."

"So, you're going to save him from Mother Nature, acts of God, and any bump and scrape from life itself?" Marsha pressed.

Feeling overtaken by the frustration of once again not being able to make headway, I shook my head. "I just don't want him to suffer." I fumed to myself. "It's plain and simple. He's my boy, and my job is to protect him from any needless bullshit."

"So," Marsha broke in, "what are you going to do now?"

Biting my lip, I childishly wallowed to myself. "I'll do what I always do, suck it up, take care of the mess, and try to keep everybody off my ass!"

As our arguments became a biweekly event, one of Marsha's statements became ingrained in my head. Once, after I again saved Patsy from another financial abyss, Marsha lashed, "I just wish you fought for me as much as you fight for them."

That statement pierced. I knew in my heart that I truly tried my absolute best. But, because I was doing so much for so long, I automatically relied on my hardwired survival mechanisms so I could focus on the task of making so many things just right. *Then*, once I felt safe, I could finally let my guard down and relax. With Marsha, in the beginning, I felt there was always another chance to make things up to her.

What I failed to comprehend was, despite my selfish need for companionship, how much Marsha had given up to be with me. I didn't realize that she was extremely homesick. That when I said the wrong thing, Marsha became triggered and would suddenly burst out in tears, crying uncontrollably for hours upon hours at a time. She seemed to have increasingly volatile highs and depressing lows.

Even though she told me, I didn't see how hard it was for Marsha. When I was on the road, she would drive across the bridge to her unheated apartment after she ended her workday and crawl into her small daybed, using layers of jackets and blankets to keep her from shivering as she cried herself to sleep. And, even though unbeknownst to her I was paying Marsha more than I paid myself, money was tight for her, and she only seemed her happiest when she went shopping.

As our bickering continued, at times it seemed an all-or-nothing contest of childlike wills.

When I was married to Patsy, my mindset was that everything she did adversely affected our marriage, while I rarely gave much thought to my own idiosyncrasies that added to our volatile mixture. Toward the end of our union, I *knew* it was *all* Patsy's fault and I *knew* that if I ever had a chance with someone else, not only would everything be easy, but perfect, because whatever issues I had with my past relationship, they surely would *never* repeat themselves.

So, this time, with Marsha, I thought if I could just fix everything, then everything would work out.

Yet, between my exhausting work and travels, the never-ending needless struggles with my Florida publisher, and trying to be with my son, when it came to Marsha, no matter how bad things became, I had to fight my instinct to internally shut down. And if I couldn't solve the situation at the exact moment, I felt I would have another opportunity to prove my worth *next* time.

But, the business was also an ongoing source of increasing tension. I was gradually gaining a foothold, getting paid some funds for full-day seminars, but the big stumbling block and a major source of our frustration always seemed to be with the publisher.

While preparing for the release of the next book, *The Lost Boy*, Marsha and I were stunned when we received notice that the publisher was initiating a new policy in which the authors were *required* to have their own works completely edited and printer-ready.

"Unbelievable," Marsha huffed. "They don't print hardback books, their PR is practically nonexistent, and now you're responsible for 'editing your own works.' It's like they're nothing but a glorified printing company. It's insane. And why, after weeks of me calling them with no response, to ask what editor they're going to assign to your next book, do they suddenly pull this?"

So, without getting sucked into another argument of quicksand, I immediately let it go and scraped funds together to properly pay Marsha to edit my second book.

Then weeks later Marsha discovered through the grapevine that after the publisher was going to print a few copies as contractually required of *The Lost Boy*, they were going to immediately cancel *A Child Called "It."* "Word is," Marsha informed me, "they believe they *carried* your first book for *way* too long."

Immediately I thought of Marsha and how much she believed in the books. I apologized to Marsha for the fact that, after all her work as an editor and taking a chance by coming out to Grudge-ville, the books would end like this.

But I knew that no matter what I said, no matter how much I tried to coat it all with as much syrup as possible, it was still a crushing blow for Marsha.

I didn't even give much thought to myself and the *years* of time and effort I had put in. For me, writing the first book was like crawling on shards of glass. So, in order to not feel enraged, all I could do was swallow another defeat and simply press on. At least I had a published book that I had mailed to my siblings and that one day I could present to my son.

Over the next few weeks, without Marsha's knowledge, I called the president of the publishing company to apologize for the lack of book sales. I even called Kerry in the PR department to apologize to her for doing anything that might have made *her* upset or that might have had an effect on the book's demise.

All the while I hoped that someone would have the courtesy to officially tell me about the book's cancellation and possibly offer an explanation for why the first book had failed—why I had failed. But all I was able to do was continue to chase something elusive. In my current pursuit, I left a string of voice mails that were never returned.

A short time later, out of the blue, I caught a break. A young television producer who had read my book wanted to do a show on overcoming adversity.

The night before the show, ensconced in my hotel room in the heart of New York City, I couldn't sleep a wink. My concern was that once I appeared on a national program, I would surely incense my grandmother. It might also upset my brothers, who were already unhappy with me and would be more displeased with me exposing our family secret for all to hear.

Back when I was in the air force and covertly began my journey in child abuse prevention, I did all I could to protect my brothers' privacy. I felt their embarrassment over what happened to us, and even sympathized with one sibling who publicly announced, "*My* mother's not like that. *She* never abused *him*."

But now, no matter what the show's outcome, I was "coming out" much more than I'd ever dared. But it was publicly venturing that close to my past, connecting me with Mother, that terrified me the most.

Taping the show was a whirlwind. The host, Montel Williams, and every member of his staff were beyond gracious. It was scary. I could not accept that after all the years of work, all the uphill battles and all the sacrifices, a television host would praise me to his audience.

Yet the question that made me lose it was when Mr. Williams sincerely probed, "All the things that you do, why? Why do you do this?"

Feeling the pent-up pressure that I had buried since my days in the basement, I had somehow forgotten about the exact intentions of my quest. Without analyzing, I blubbered something to the effect of, "I know what it's like to have nothing, to be less than zero. When my teachers risked everything to step up and intervene, there's no doubt in my mind that they saved my life. When someone saves you, it never goes away. So, I feel that I owe this debt. The least I can do is pay back and somehow leave a cleaner footprint on this planet, for my son, and so others won't have to suffer."

By the time I finished my blathering, disjointed statement, I found myself overwhelmed to the point of tears. As embarrassed as I was, I couldn't control the floodgates. Off camera during the commercial break, the host was emotional too. Without a word, we hugged each other.

Afterward, to my complete surprise, Montel brought out my teachers, Mr. Ziegler and Mrs. Woodworth, who both explained what it was like for them to have to deal with my extreme, dysfunctional behavior, my mother's paper thin justifications, which they knew were complete fabrications, and how my situation wore heavily on *their* hearts.

When my once seemingly hard-core, no-nonsense fifth grade homeroom teacher, Mr. Ziegler, stated, "I should have, could have, done more—and that's something *I* have to live with." I lost it all over again.

With all my years of reliving and dissecting all that happened with Mother and me, I had never reflected on what my teachers carried with them in the private recesses of their own hearts. Sitting next to my saviors, I became aware of their years of unspoken, protective love for not only a mistreated child such as myself, but for all of the other children under their years of guardianship.

Within a short time of the show's airing, *A Child Called "It,"* much to the astonishment of some of the staff of the publishing company, began to take off. I was ecstatic. But as over the moon as I was about the book, I switched off any excitement. Everything remained as it had been before: I continued to travel, then when home, I fought to balance my time between keeping up with the escalating mounds of paperwork and various requests, being with Stephen, and *then* spending time with Marsha.

But month by month as I lost more time, Marsha and I became more strained. If anything, as my workload steadily increased, Marsha slowly required more and more time off. There always seemed to be a sudden reason for her to fly off to visit her relatives back in Florida.

The tension kept building until one afternoon when Marsha and I argued so badly that she flew out early for a preplanned visit home. Licking my wounds over yet another eruption, I thought it best to give Marsha as much space as possible. I only called her once to make sure that she had safely arrived in her home state.

About two weeks later, during the last week of October, I left home at one a.m. to drive eleven hours, nearly nonstop, south to Palm Springs, where I was to give a presentation.

Less than two days after that, again in the very early morning hours, I piloted my Toyota from Palm Springs to Los Angeles for a jam-packed day of scheduled events.

As much as things seemed to be on the verge of breaking for me, my concern was to remain completely emotionally disconnected and direct my entire focus to making sure I had the precise directions. I could not allow myself to become even slightly intoxicated by the mere whiff of fairy-tale possibilities.

Arriving way too early in west LA, I cruised south on Main Street in Santa Monica, stopping at the local Starbucks, which had just opened for the day. As I left with a small coffee in hand, I came across a homeless gentleman. Our eyes met and we simultaneously smiled. I felt the man's gesture had absolutely nothing to do with seeking pity or searching for some form of handout. I returned into the coffee shop, ordered a grande cup of coffee and a couple of scones. I then secretly placed a bill into the bag before bowing slightly as I gave the man his gift.

Something in his eyes reminded me of my father, the courageous firefighter, whose badge I carried at that very moment. The man standing outside of Starbucks had the same posture, piercing eyes, and the strong sense of pride. Under the cover of still-darkened skies, the encounter made me think back to my youth in foster care, how I used to pray with intensity that someone might be kind enough to help my father, whom I feared was homeless on the cold streets of San Francisco.

The man spilled over with thanks. I nodded to say it was okay. As I began to walk away, the elderly gentleman grabbed the arm of my jacket with his thick, reddened hand.

"You'll be blessed," he announced with conviction as he held on. "You'll see. You're a good son."

Later, as I drove away in the security and the warmth of my 4Runner, the man's words continued to resonate. Of all things, with all my endless—and at times repetitive—faults, at my core, I simply wanted to be good. To be that good person, and from the heavens above, for my father to see and feel within his own troubled soul how I yearned to be *that* good son.

Hours later, during an extended break, I made a fast call to leave the usual message for Kerry at the publisher to check on my sales standing. For the last few weeks, because the publisher, for some odd reason, could not fill the orders to the chain of distributors, which fed directly into the bookstores, my sales, which had jumped initially, were now steadily declining. I was surprised when Kerry actually took my call, and I knew by her kind hello that something was up.

"Glad you caught me," Kerry said in a chipper voice. "Was just going to head out for lunch. Anyway, I was going to try to call you. You're number fourteen on the *New York Times* best-seller list!"

Overwhelmed by something I had never thought remotely possible, I excitedly thanked Kerry and everyone else for all their support. Then I immediately called the two ladies from the sales department who had always been genuinely supportive and kind since the day the book was first submitted. Ireena gushed with pride, "Think about it, your book was printed in '93, published in late '95 and *now*, four years later, you make it on the list!"

As Ireena and I blathered about the first book's nearly doomed journey (which both Dick and Kerry had yet to mention), Ireena said she found it odd that no one, especially Dick, the president, had bothered to call me to announce the good news.

As my feelings of gratitude formed into words, I immediately thought of Marsha. With time running short, I called Marsha's cell phone but it was off, so I instantly called her parents' house. Her mother answered the phone, initially sounding cold and distant, but once I broke the news, her demeanor suddenly changed.

With my break almost over, I raced to pay respects to one more person. Since Jimmy, the producer with Montel Williams, wasn't available, his boss, Alex, took the call. Before I could tell him the news, Alex congratulated me.

"Sir," I began, "my publishers were going to cancel the book. It was on the chopping block."

Alex sighed. "Yeah, I know."

I stated, "I just need you, Mr. Williams, and everyone else to know that you folks made it into a best seller."

"Now, now," Alex cut me off, "I wouldn't go as far as that. You gave us a good show and you've got a story with universal appeal. Don't limit yourself."

As always, I heard but didn't receive the kind gesture. "No sir!" I deflected, knowing how blessed I was with the timing of all the elements. "The simple fact is that all of you believed in what the book and I really stood for. I didn't have to fight, or chase, or prove... I just can't begin to tell you, after all these years, all the bullshit... what *that* means to me!" I stumbled to finish. "Thank you, sir!"

Hours later, I drove to meet with a movie producer. I had fantasized about driving onto the lot of a major studio and walking down the same hallways as those who made movie magic. But, after driving north on the California freeway and snaking my way through a very run-down neighborhood, I nearly gasped when the producer and his eager assistant met me at the front door of his dilapidated house. I knew I was in trouble when the three of us held our meeting in the producer's garage, which he had almost converted into an office.

All the while as the supposed *producer* bragged about how influential he was, as the young assistant parroted every other sentence to hammer in the point, I shook my head, thinking, "How in heaven's name do *I* keep attracting the same type of people? How come I'm not good enough? What am I doing wrong?"

But as the two men yammered away, I knew the answer. Even with all the blessings and all of my success, I simply didn't believe *I* deserved better. I got what I sought—what I saw within myself.

After my garage meeting, I immediately drove back to southern Santa Monica to meet with Wanda, the owner of a speakers' bureau. But in the time it took me to shake hands, I knew by the familiar dispirited gaze that my hopes were once again about to be dashed.

"Listen," Wanda sighed as if confessing. "I'm sorry, but it's not going to happen. We don't get many calls, actually, any calls, for victims of child abuse. And, I *know* you've said you're not about abuse, but after rereading your book, I can't help it. I still see you as that little boy, and I'm afraid others will too. I really don't see your story breaking through, it's just too grim. As much as you say others pass it around, it certainly doesn't have the making of a best seller. Of course, if it did, that would be a different story. *Maybe* then I just might be able to use you."

For the second time, in the span of a few hours, I somehow had the sense to not try to prove the book's success, to chase after this lady's approval to no avail. As much as I wanted to remind Wanda of our numerous conversations in which she had stressed how she had been searching for someone who personified overcoming obstacles and being of public service, luckily, I kept my big trap shut.

In the end I hugged Wanda and told her that I would put her in my prayers, as she had just disclosed that she was in treatment for cancer and had decided, that very day, to sell her company so she could have enough to pay her escalating bills.

Later, as my Toyota lurched a whopping five feet in the middle of all the traffic, I suddenly lost my energy from the day's events. I had planned to push myself (as always) and drive nonstop back to Guerneville. But after progressing a mere mile in just under an hour, without analyzing the cost, or how much time I would lose by not starting work early the next morning, I exited the freeway and checked into a hotel.

Inside the stuffy room, I wrung a hot washcloth and scrubbed away the layers of grime from my face. Suddenly feeling as if I had finished back-to-back multiple marathons, I nearly stumbled as I made my way to the west-facing window. I flung open the curtains before opening the long rectangular window. For a few seconds I stood simply absorbing LA's warm, crisp air as the last gleaming orange rays of the sun shone off the tops of the nearby buildings. Remembering that I had repeatedly set aside my reward of getting anything to eat that entire day, I succumbed to exhaustion.

Ever so slowly, I knelt down on both knees in front of the pane of glass, and I cried. After the initial rush of receiving the news of the book's success, now in my hotel room, I felt more alone than I had even before I had met Marsha.

CHAPTER 14

OF ALL THINGS

I WORE MY WEDDING BAND for the longest time after Marsha and I were divorced. And every time I studied my ring, a searing feeling of shame shot up my spine. Once that sensation abated, it was followed by a blanket of immense sadness. Over the last several months, at least four or five times a day, I'd twirl the band before playfully pulling it from my finger. I had a hard time letting go.

Early one morning while nursing a cold cup of coffee, I stared up at a collage that Marsha had put together at the far end of the kitchen. It displayed photos of Marsha and me, with her three dogs dressed in various silly outfits and her chirpy, exotic bird. Nearly a full year after separating, in part because of my fear of the unknown road ahead, I refused to take it down. But at least, I mused to myself, I did cover up some of the photos.

Without thought, I plucked a photo from the display. Leaning back while unconsciously spinning my ring, as sad as I was, I was able to smile at a moment of my past.

The picture seemed like a lifetime ago. I stood relaxed with smiling eyes next to a gigantic original Italian version of the movie poster for *The Good, The Bad and The Ugly*. It was the very day I had become a best-selling author. A day full of intense emotional highs and lows. Yet the single theme that I remembered was how I didn't *allow* myself to feel much elation. My reasoning was that I always felt I did not deserve any joy. And whenever anything good happened, soon enough, something horribly bad would take its place. So, in the long run, it was simply better not to expect too much.

Spinning my ring on the top of the breakfast table, I seemed to take in much more joy from the picture now than I had back in the day.

I also recalled how intensely insane my life suddenly became.

By the time I returned to Guerneville from the LA area, my fax machine had run out of paper, my voice mail was full, and the phone rang nonstop. Struggling to catch up, I'd take notes of the messages, yet most of them were long, rambling, and completely incoherent. In one series, a frantic woman screamed how *they* were after her, how she had no idea where she was, and how I needed to immediately find her and protect her from life-threatening harm. The telephone booth lady, as I dubbed her, called several times a night, adding increased intensity to her plight. Yet in less than a week the lady's attitude changed as she screeched that I was just like the others and how she would now hunt me down and make me feel all the pain that I had deliberately caused her.

In another series of messages, a man stated how he too was going to hunt me down because he had heard me on a radio show, and because he was a Vietnam veteran, he "knew the truth."

After a few hours, overwhelmed and bewildered, all I could do was rest my pencil from taking notes and scan through the rest of the recordings. I closed my eyes against all the pain that spewed from the machine. If anything, I thought to myself, I was thankful that Marsha was still on vacation and didn't have to hear any of the filth.

But within mere moments of the next message, I sprang forward, hearing the voice of my grandmother. "Whatever you're doing, *you* call *me* this very instant!" Thinking of her old age and health issues, I contemplated the worst. Yet when I returned the call, I learned Grandmother's message had nothing to do with her being in need.

Without even returning a salutation, Gram lit into me. "Just what in the hell do you think you're doing? I've called you twice in two days, twice. Whenever I call, you pick up that damn phone. hell's bells." Grandmother huffed. Switching gears, she then berated me, "Do you know what you've done? Do you? So, what do you have to say for yourself, young man?"

With the phone pressed against my ringing ear, I shook my head no. I knew, just like with Mother, that whatever I said, it would be taken the wrong way and only set Grandmother off all the more. After a few seconds of Gram breathing heavily into the phone, she flung, "When I ask you a question, you better well answer." A heartbeat later, Grandmother stated, "It seems that alligator mouth of yours has overloaded your canary ass. And if I told you once, I've told you a million times to keep your dirty laundry to yourself..."

I shook my head; *now* I knew why Gram had called. Even though she'd had my two printed books for several years, the popularity of *A Child Called "It"* made my grandmother beyond livid.

"I want you to know that I've read a few more pages from *that* book. If you ask me, it seems more like fiction. I just don't see how she could do any of those things to you. It makes no sense." Knowing how Grandmother had stated the same sentiment about what had transpired between Mother and me since my days in foster care, all I could do was nod my head and wait for the next round of mortar fire.

And, as always, I knew her rants against me really had to do with how my past made her appear. "I'm certainly not saying it happened, and I'm not saying it didn't. Anyhow..."

With my mouth clamped shut, I wanted to declare, "For God's sake, as much as you lay into everyone, telling them what you think, and what they should do, why, now, can't you decide? And, if it didn't happen, why were *you* the one who called Child Protective Services in the first place? Why in the hell do you think I was so suddenly taken away, huh?"

As if on cue, Grandmother unknowingly steamrolled over my internal rhetorical questions by saying, "The way I heard it, that mother of yours, well, she told me that March when she came over with the kids on *my* birthday, that *you* were taken away because, because, well, you burnt down your school—the entire school. At least, that's what she said."

That was the exact same thing, word for word, that my brother, Stan had said when we had unexpectedly met while at Parkside Junior High School, when I was in foster care with the Turnbough family. In part because my younger brother suffered from Bell's palsy and because Mother seemed overly devoted to him, Stan, who had always cherished Mother, *wanted* to believe every malicious thing, no matter how ridiculously outrageous, stated against me.

Thankfully, in a matter of just a few days, I felt in my heart that Stan, in his own way, had come to know the truth. While at Parkside, every recess break we were as we had been back in the days of elementary school before everything turned so divisive and dark—inseparable.

"Burned down the school, the entire school?" I rolled my eyes. "Okay, so why wasn't I arrested? Why wasn't it the talk of the town? Why didn't it make the news? Or," I huffed, "where did all these kids go the next day, unless, hello, there was never any fire? Grandma, come on," I gently inserted, "now, you know that's not true. My God, it's just so obvious..."

"Doesn't matter!" Grandmother broke in.

"Sorry, I don't... what do you mean?" I asked. "That Mother lied about the school being burned or...?"

"It doesn't matter, because you can never believe anything that comes out of her mouth, ever!"

Catching on, as if we had both stumbled onto some psychological breakthrough, I stammered, "Okay, so you're saying that you knew all along that Mom was lying, that she was just making up all those... excuses? *You* actually knew?" I probed, feeling a sigh of relief and sense of pride that *finally* Grandmother acknowledged that I wasn't this despicable *thing* that Mother had conjured up to every living person for all those years.

Huffing as if I were an immense strain, Grandmother flung back, "I'm not saying I knew about *anything* and I'm not saying that I didn't! All I am saying is none of it, none of it should matter—period!"

Grandmother's confessional statement bounced inside my head. "I'll tell you what," Gram plowed on. "Your problem is that you never think of anybody but your own damn self—never! Did you ever give a thought, before telling the world your tale of woe," Grandmother paused before her pitch changed to a higher level, "about *me*? Did you even think about how I might feel if anyone ever came up to me and asked about Roerva Catherine as my daughter from your little tome? How do you think all this makes me look?

"I told you a long time ago to watch your step and not involve anyone in any of your doings. Don't you think that you have brought enough shame to this family, hm? And, didn't I tell you that you shouldn't have had that piece of filth published in the first place? It seems to me that your brothers and you never paid any attention to any damn thing I've ever said, the whole lot of you! Not you kids and especially not her. And I'm just sick of everything, and everybody. Sick, sick, sick. You just better pray that that book of yours is just some passing fancy, 'cause if it's not, I'll tell you what I'm going to do, I'm going to dish out my two cents and..."

My split second of breaking common ground and feeling just a step closer to my elder suddenly came out from under my feet. "So," I analyzed to myself, "nothing matters. After all the absolute hell your daughter put all of us through in part because 'you knew or didn't know,' at the end of the day, the only thing that does matter is *you*?!"

Knowing Gram's pattern of spewing on for hours without coming up for air, I rushed a quick good-bye and hung up before she could launch her volley against me, my siblings, and the world at large.

Tapping my fingers on the picture, I reconnected to how sick I felt from all the gut-wrenching tension and how I just sat on my rump, taking in all the disgusting, verbal hatred that Gram flung out.

"And yet," I exhaled to myself while increasing the rhythm of my fingers, "what if there was an ounce of truth in what Grandmother stated?" Taking a moment to reflect, I realized I had never given much thought when working on the book to how my mother's behavior would make Grandmother appear, and all the pain it may have caused Gram from the process. As a parent myself, I could not begin to imagine the mere thought of how I would react if *I* had a child who grew up to become "absolute evil." Yet, at the very least, there was absolutely no doubt in my heart that I would do all I could to repair any damage caused by my offspring. But, in Grandmother's defense, I knew that she was too proud to admit Mother's sickness, in part because Gram was raised in the era of kept secrets and therefore truly *believed* that certain problems, no matter how extensive or horrid, should be kept "in the house."

And, to be brutally honest, while I did want the book to succeed because I *was* in part selfishly proud of it and truly believed it might help the cause of preventing child abuse, in a million years, I never meant for *A Child Called "It"* to bring shame to my grandmother and especially not to my estranged brothers.

But obviously, I realized, it did. And, as promised, I did all I could to protect my siblings' privacy and never gave out any addresses or phone numbers, although the press would somehow find and pester each of them. One malicious person took advantage of Stan, and when I read the piece with his quotes, my insides dissolved.

As much as I wanted to rip into Stan for saying I made everything up, even telling the journalist that I was *dishonorably* discharged from the air force, I cooled it because I had put him in a tough spot. Only after I hung up from speaking with him about the article and looked at my notes did I see it. Over and over, Stan had stated, *his* mom. He never saw *his* mom do anything, and *his* mom wasn't really like that.

"For God's sake, Stan, remember how Mom would make up all that stuff, like the time she said I murdered somebody, or that I had burned down the school?"

"She was always saying stuff," Stan said. "You know how Mom got when she was pissed off and drank too much."

I concluded that Stan believed (or wanted to) that *his mom* was a different person than the terror that she actually was! And, just as I had disassociated when I was abused, perhaps Stan, in his own way, did the same.

In the end, I knew how much Stan loved his mother and how devastated he was when she unexpectedly died in her sleep in January of '92. I also knew how incredibly devoted he was to her. Thinking back, I remembered in the summer of '78, when I was selling cars at Serramonte

Ford, just outside his hometown of Daly City, and I discovered Stan walking just across from the car lot. After running to meet him, Stan proudly stated that he had landed a job at a Burger King a few cities over and how he was going to use his earnings to surprise his mother with a brand-new color television set. I couldn't believe how much of an effort it must have been for Stan to walk over an hour, up and down the various hills, just to catch a bus so he could do something for Mother.

And, I recalled, a few years back, when I spoke to my eldest brother, Ron, a veteran patrol officer in the Midwest; Ron tore into me, telling me that once when he pulled over a vehicle, the driver became excited, asking Officer Pelzer if he were indeed related to the guy who wrote *A Child Called "It."* The part that had stunned me was how embarrassed he said he was to be my brother.

Plucking another photo from the collage, I sighed when I realized, once again, without ever intending to, I had made others suffer through my own conduct. With a mounting sadness beginning to fill me, I sat back and crumbled photo after photo in my vise-like grip.

Staring at the growing pile of pictures, I felt ice-cold. For the first time in my life I became consumed with complete loss and was without a sense of hope. The sensation had been creeping within me for several months, but somehow I had been able to stay ahead of its grasp by running away through my personal cause. And now, as parts of my past were laid in front of me, all I could feel was dread.

Plucking off one last picture, which happened to be of Marsha, I hissed at my delusional conviction that no matter what happened, I could weed away every problem that suddenly sprang up. That I had enough time for another chance to prove my worth and in the end everything would be all the better, and I could then lower my layers of shields and finally relax and stop my lifelong running.

But the pyramid-shaped evidence of my past told a different story.

After Marsha returned to California, instead of confronting our differences, we immediately returned to hiding behind our work and its baffling situations that only escalated by the day.

It never ended, and there was always *something*.

Gazing down at the pictures, I knew we'd both tried. And many years after we had first met; after we married thinking that would bring us closer together; after I fled from Guerneville to buy my wife a brand-new home in Southern California, enabling her to purchase items that I thought would make her less despondent and somehow happy; after she finally returned from yet another unexpected, lengthy vacation with huge boxes from her latest spree that filled the living room; and after a great deal of soul searching, I had announced my intentions of divorce.

With the purest of emotions, Marsha had exhaled. She'd truly seemed relieved.

Feeling the sudden need to hide under the covers of my bed, I swiped the small pile of photos to the floor. When I did, I could hear the slight clinking sound of my ring at the bottom of the mound. I didn't have the compassion to retrieve it.

CHAPTER 15

A CHANGE IN CIRCUMSTANCE

IT WASN'T A SUDDEN THING. There was no magical, climactic moment. Nor was it some invisible weight that was abruptly lifted. But, one afternoon as I sat still, staring aimlessly at the backyard, I consciously noticed that I no longer felt that deep, massive pain over the loss of my failed marriage or the lead-blanket shame of my past.

As I studied the brightly colored flowers that I had recently meticulously planted, I realized that I may have found the bridge that led to a path of acceptance.

Drawing fresh air into my lungs, I knew that day by day, if only for a few more minutes or even a few scant seconds, I felt just a bit more peace within myself than I had the day before. And while I wanted, craved, and fought myself for more solace, I was learning to submit to the process, which made me all the more grateful.

I had always prided myself in being grateful, in part because I had begun to take an inventory of my own issues. And as slimy as it made me feel, in the long haul, it gave me a deeper sense of appreciation of the life with which I had been blessed.

I was learning that I didn't *have to* do all things all the time and that I didn't have to suddenly solve everyone's problems in order to give myself validation. And while I still was committed to helping others, I no longer carried everyone on my back. I was beginning to form boundaries.

And, I was learning to be truer to myself by taking the chance to quit feeling suppressed and actually speak my mind. At times, I'd make a mistake with my fast-quip humor or advice. However, I knew my heart was in the right place.

Smiling at myself, I recalled how that very day I'd had the rare opportunity to have a lengthy conversation with my eldest brother, and I could hardly believe my ears. On the other end of the phone line, Ron was doing something I had never heard him do before: open up and purge.

"You'd think that after all the years my wife and I have gone out of our way to help Gram out, that the least she could do is be nice? She knows I don't get any time off and it takes me seventeen hours just to make the drive. Then the moment we arrive, forget about unpacking, oh no, Linda and I have to do everything, the housework, the shopping, bathing her, even helping her go to the bathroom. And it's always the same, every visit, every day, bitch, bitch, bitch. The whole thing makes me so pissed."

Jumping in, in a flat tone, I asked my respected elder brother, "Then… why do you do it?"

I knew the answer. When it came to chasing after Mother's approval, I was like an addict who was fighting to stay in recovery—I could only work out my problems one day at a time, stay busy, keep my side of the street clean, and all the while keep the Serenity Prayer close to my heart.

Being more than curious, I wondered if my brother really knew why he put himself and his tremendously kind wife through so much needless abuse. Maybe he didn't know. Maybe, because he had been doing it for so long, it all seemed natural for him. Or maybe it was that Ron, like me in some ways, was very old-school about respecting his elders and being of service. Still, I sensed it was more about old wounds that he still carried.

I definitely related.

Having tossed out my imperative question and hearing no response, I switched to being supportive. "Ron, you, *sir*, don't need to do it. After all these years, ten, fifteen, whatever the number, you have to know, Gram's never going to change. It's her world. She's always going to be toxic. She's a mean, bitter person who feeds off of making others feel her pain. I know you know this!" I deliberately stopped to allow my statement to sink in. On the other end I could hear Ron exhale, as if he were agreeing. "I'm in no way trying to be disrespectful here, but Gram is 'The Darkness.'"

I paused again to solidify my connection. "Russell and Kevin were too young, but you remember how Gram used to come over and try and take over Mom's house when the three of us were just kids, the way she used to run down Mom right in front of us or yell at her on the phone for hours on end? Gram did it 'cause that's what she loves. Believe me, I'm not excusing Mom's behavior, but Gram has to take some of that responsibility."

"You don't know the half of it," Ron said. "I always told you... you were the lucky one. When you took off, it's like they both became crazier."

I closed my eyes as if to hide behind my emotional shield. Not a single day slipped past that I did not feel for my brothers and the toll it must have taken on them to live with Mother's wounded rage.

When Mother passed away, the five of us came together for the first time as brothers. We spent nearly a week cleaning out her trashed-out house. During that time, Ron had made the same off-the-cuff remark a few times (which I took as nothing more than nervous ribbing) about me being *lucky*. As excited as I was to be with my brothers, a small part of me became upset for holding in what I felt all those darkened years.

For a mere moment, as much as I respected my oldest sibling, I had wanted to stop Ron dead in his tracks and ask, "Just what in the hell planet are you from? Lucky? When I had to sit on my hands until they were numb at the bottom of the basement stairs, cold and starving, while you guys gorged yourselves with hot, fresh-cooked dinners, was *that* me being lucky? Or when I was everyone's slave, doing the dishes, scrubbing the toilet bowl, or cleaning out the cat box with my fingers, for the mere chance of maybe getting leftovers after the dogs picked through them, was that luck? What about sleeping in the basement on that army cot and using rags to wrap around my feet, or forced to swallow ammonia, and eating dog shit, while you guys played outside? Or how 'bout when you, Stan, and Russell used to take turns kicking me around like a soccer ball? Is that what you call lucky?

"I didn't 'take off,'" I continued in my mind. "I was removed, taken away. I know you went through a lot, all of you! But, when I left, you were thirteen, not four, when Mom went crazy on me. I'm not trying to compare, but you have no idea how f'ing scared I was back then, and I mean every moment of every day, or the hell I went through trying to adjust to all those foster homes.

"I know in the beginning she did her best to brainwash you and Stan. Then, by the time I was in the second, third grade, I knew, hey man, it's life in the food chain. And, I know that after Dad left things got even more crazy worse and I was an embarrassment, some sideshow freak everyone knew about but no one ever spoke of. I don't blame anybody but Mom. But lucky? Please."

But now, as a middle-aged man coming to terms with my flaws and failures, I kept my mouth shut, thinking it was more important for me to simply focus on my side of the street.

Yet with Ron it was always difficult. Of all the brothers, I felt it was Ron who kept it all in and suffered the worst. And even though he never spoke of the situation, the unique gifts he had given me over the years screamed volumes—a metal police car with the inscription *Daly City Police Department*, a cookbook of Mother's unique recipes, and, the crème de la crème, a photo album that Ron had put together showing Mother as a small girl along with a series of pictures of her as a young woman, skiing, fishing, and even chopping wood. There were also photos of our very young parents, smiling and dancing as they celebrated in the garage of their new home. And then the ones of Mother holding Ron as a newborn, then myself, and then Stan.

For endless hours, I would study every aspect of every person and every item in the pictures as if there was a clue to how things came to be. Then one afternoon, I saw it—a shift in Mother's gaze as she held baby Stan on her lap. In all the other photos, she had a gleam in her eyes, a radiance that seemed to surround her face. But after having given birth to three kids in less than four years, her expression seemed to announce, "The party's over."

On the phone, I reached out to my brother about something that we both loved. "So, do you ever think you'll come back to California? Do you ever think you'll see Guerneville again?"

Hearing the heavy sigh on the other end, I immediately knew the answer. We had talked about his coming out to visit for over a decade. "Well, I'd like to see that beach by Daly City."

"The one near where Uncle Hap used to keep his horses?" I reminisced with him.

"Yeah," my big brother said a quick second later.

"And the Golden Gate Bridge, and the park where Mom used to drive us on John F. Kennedy Drive, and up around Stow Lake and Rainbow Falls and Steinhart Aquarium where you, Stan, and I used to run past the doors so we could press our noses against the brass seahorse-shaped railing that overlooked the alligator pit." Becoming excited about possible bonding, I sped off, "I took my Stephen to the park dozens of times when he was our age. I got photos of him by the giant waterfall."

"Yeah, I know. I know. You told me that, before." I felt I was losing him.

Fishing for a strand, I said, "Did I tell you they rebuilt the whole aquarium? It's so different, it's like, New Agey. I mean, it's okay, but I just like the way it used to be, that look, the feel of that era."

"They still have 'the pit?'" Ron sincerely asked.

I could feel that thread of connection. "Kinda. They still have the brass seahorses. They kept 'em. It was a huge thing, everybody wanted to have that…" Suddenly I stumbled, looking for the precise word. Then I smiled. "Connection to that time… maybe, their childhoods." I stopped, almost shuddering at my discovery. "So," I came back around, "you gonna come out?"

"I don't know, man. I dunno." As he stopped, the energy behind his words seemed to drain. "Hey, man, I gotta…"

"I know," I quickly replied.

"Take care, man."

I smiled at his salutation. "And you too. God bless."

After placing the phone receiver into its cradle, I strongly felt that Ron would never again see a California sunset with his own eyes. Back when the books were on the best-seller list, I had proudly offered Ron and his family to come out as my guests. I had it all planned: I would drive them through Golden Gate Park and then across the Golden Gate Bridge, until we all arrived at Guerneville. I would have given anything to see the expression on Ron's face as we slowly made our way down Main Street. But as the years piled up, there was always some barrier—work, kids, and the one that seemed most paramount, time.

At the very least, in a few of our conversations, we had regained a sliver of that feeling we'd had when we were close as brothers. One of these moments of closeness for me was when our parents took Ron, Stan, and me on a picnic at nearby Junipero Serra Park: after wolfing down our deviled ham sandwiches, Ron had begged Mother and Father to let him take Stan and me up an unpaved hill, completely on our own. At first Mother had adamantly refused. But Father, who trusted his oldest son, gave his blessing by patting Ron on the shoulder. "Make sure you look after your two brothers."

When we got to the base of the hill, it seemed taller than Mt. Everest. A few feet into our climb, Stan and I were huffing and puffing away, losing our footing and all our energy, while Ron, leading the way, stood perfectly tall without a bead of sweat. As we reached the mighty summit, my foot slipped and I could feel myself sliding backward. With momentum beginning to take over, I knew I would collide with Stan, and together the both of us would be hurled off the hill and would certainly perish.

Sliding on my butt, I could see the terror in Stan's eyes, yet before I could let out a cry, I felt a sudden jolt on my right arm. While Stan grabbed my left foot, I stared up at Ron, who with the sun's rays just behind him seemed to have the exact hair color of my other hero, Father. He gave me a nonchalant smile. With one word, my brother said it all. "Gotcha."

CHAPTER 16

THE PASSING OF THE POSSIBILITY

ONE DAY, OUT OF THE BLUE, I got the call. Before my youngest brother, Kevin, could get the words out, I knew. "Gram's dead," he choked. Sitting outside in the comfort of the descending autumn sun, I felt, oddly enough, as if some weight had been lifted. Speaking slowly but also carefully, I asked, "How you doing, Kev?"

Ever a gentle soul, he chuckled. "You know, I always said that for Gram heaven was not an option and hell wouldn't take her either. But the funny thing is, now, I don't know. I'm going to miss her."

Thinking of all the emotional conversations I'd had with Kevin over the years about how much pain Grandma had deliberately caused him and his wife, and how she went out of her way to disrespect his children, Kevin's genuine sincerity always rose above it all.

"A hundred years," Kevin stated. "Can you imagine living that long?"

I nodded my head in absolute agreement. "I gotta tell ya, Kev, I so wish I was friends with her. Can you imagine asking Gram what was it like to see her first car, her first movie as a kid, or what it was like to see a biplane fly over and then, years later, to fly in a jet? My God, think about it, running water, toilets! I wonder if Gram ever went to an IMAX show in 3-D… or surfed the Internet. Man, imagine the stories she could tell."

My voice trailed off, and I thought to myself, "What a waste. All that time consumed with so much hate, for what? Against what? A hundred years walking on this earth—what a legacy."

The next day I was able to reach Stan. Of the five of us, he would take Grandmother's passing the hardest. "With Mom gone and now Gram, I just don't know…" he confessed.

With physical and emotional distance, I replayed some of the talks Stan and I had when he, like Ron and Kevin, could never do enough for Grandmother, and how Stan craved a kind word, just once, a single compliment, which he never received.

"Stan," I said to get his full attention. "I need you to hear this."

Inside my heart I added, "I really need you to *receive* this."

"Stan, *you* were a good grandson. You did so much for Gram for many, many years. You, Ron, and Kev, you all did the right thing. I know you're going to miss her, but now it's time for you to do what you need to do for you, rather than doing so much for everyone else. It's your time. And, Stan," I deliberately slowed my pace, "you deserve to be happy and be around those who make you happy. Stan… you above all *deserve*. Do you hear me?"

To myself, I pleaded, "Am I getting through?"

Stan acknowledged what I said, but I knew it was too much for him to truly take in and it would take some time to process. We talked about seeing each other in a few days and I offered to take us all out for dinner. "Even Russell?" Stan laughed.

"Yeah, even Russell, no worries." I laughed along with him. "And Stan, one more thing, lay off that Jägermeister."

The next Saturday at Grandmother's service, my brothers and some of their family members sat in the front row. By choice, I stood in the very back with my niece's husband, Dennis, a kind man who toiled constantly but could never get ahead, and whom I had not seen since Patsy and I had visited Grandmother one Thanksgiving when my son, Stephen, was still a toddler.

During the service a young woman spoke about her family's "adopted" grandmother and how generous, kind, and loving Grandmother was to her family.

Dennis and I nudged each other in the side. "Are we at the right service?" he joked.

Other members of Grandmother's "adopted" family stood up and paid tribute with stories of trips to exotic Maui and about Gram being such a stickler about golf. Yet the real surprise was that they mentioned how "difficult" she was with her own relatives.

"Jeez," I cussed under my breath while thinking of my poor brothers sitting in the front row. I wasn't upset about what had been said, or jealous about Grandmother's trips to Hawaii with no one from her biological family—no. I was completely stunned that others openly knew about

Grandmother's seething bitterness toward her own grandchildren.

Afterward at a lunch provided by the church, my brothers and I crowded around a circular table. By choice I made very little small talk. I wanted instead to observe.

When a certain relative sat down, the energy seemed to go cold. As the reminiscing started back up, someone asked the relative to tell the "cat story." Without blinking the relative regaled us, in some parts actually laughing, about coming to work very late, quite drunk and high, and how the boss yelled at my relative. So, as an act of revenge, the relative found the boss's cat, put it into a microwave, and pushed the button.

When I heard the words come out as effortlessly and as plainly as if ordering a fast-food burger to go, with absolutely no remorse, I nearly coughed up my food. It reminded me of the times I sat down and spoke to perpetrators, especially with pedophiles, who were utterly disconnected from any semblance of humanity. They even seemed to go out of their way to justify their behavior. It also made me think of the one time when I was a young man and spent several hours interviewing my mother; she too was completely disconnected while constantly defending her treatment against "*It.*"

A few hours later, Kevin and his wife were gracious enough to have everyone over for hamburgers. As Kevin flipped the burgers in the corner of his porch, I stood by listening to Ron and Russell spin tales about some of their rambunctious activities when they lived in Daly

City, California. "I'm sure they threw a party when the Pelzers left," Ron joked.

I was glad that at least it wasn't all mayhem and terror living with Mother, and that they had been old enough to temporarily escape.

The stories then veered to when Mother moved to the Salt Lake City area and the incidents in which Stan tried to rewire the downstairs bedrooms and how the brothers were fearful of fires being started. At the time, Stan had been convinced by Mother's constant praise that he was the Bob Vila of the family, and armed with nothing but raw determination, he could fix anything. I could tell by Stan's quietness and slumped shoulders that without meaning to, Ron and Russell had bruised Stan's feelings.

Straining to discover things I never knew about my brothers and how they interacted with each other, I leaned over. Ron, catching my gaze, mistook my body language. "Hey," he snapped, "you weren't no angel!"

The outside patio became dead silent. Without even meaning to, within a nanosecond, I spoke up for myself. Without thinking, I spewed, "Yeah, you're right. I *stole* food!"

A short time later, back at my hotel, emotionally drained and confused, I made a couple of calls. One of them to my new executive director, Mrs. Kathee Estey, whom I playfully called Mrs. C.

"How are ya doing?" she began.

With my right hand beginning to tremble, I opened up. "I feel like I just want to rip off my clothes, huddle in the corner, and cry."

I sometimes referred to her as the fictional character M from the James Bond series—tough as nails, but with a maternal side. "Not what you thought it would be," she stated more than asked.

Gaining control of my hand, I admitted. "Not even close."

"Never is, and it never will be." She stopped as if to let the words sink in. "What was it that you were looking for?"

"I just thought that when she finally passed away, that things would be different. That maybe we could all begin again. I'd have them all out to California, take 'em all to Guerneville, show 'em Johnson's Beach, the old house, and the tree stump where we all played." I stopped myself as I realized how consumed I was with my *own* delusional fantasy.

"*Still* trying to fix everything for everyone," I scolded myself. "Are you learning *yet*?!"

Taking in a clean breath of fresh air as I watched families take their gleeful children by the hand across the street to the theater to see the play *The Lion King*, I finished with, "I just thought, just always *believed* that since I was the *source* of it all, that I could, that I *should*, be the one to..." I stopped when I caught myself.

I then apologized for blubbering so much and thanked Mrs. C for all her prayers. In bed, as always, I said a special prayer for my brothers, whom over time and circumstances, I never really knew.

That evening in my dream, even though I was surrounded by complete darkness, I knew exactly where I stood. With perfect clarity, I could hear the trickling echo from the water spill over the smooth rocks. Within a blink of my eyes, I could now see the fallen log perched just a few feet above the water.

If my dreams of Guerneville represented my connection to my father, then the log resting at Memorial Park definitely symbolized my yearning for Mother.

Unlike the other times, I was not afraid. Beside me, I could feel Mother's presence. As the sensation grew, I remained calm, somehow knowing she was not a threat.

I kept my eyes locked on the log, waiting for my mother and the childhood me to appear. I craved the moment in which she would lovingly pull me toward her. After all these years and all that I have been so blessed to experience, I still longed to hear that precious string of words, to take in my mother's scent or feel the tickling sensation of her hair on my small face.

But mother and child did not materialize while I remained frozen on the opposite side of the fallen tree.

With the slightest of thoughts, I wished for Mother to move from beside to just in front of me. As if floating, she appeared exactly where I desired. She nodded slightly, the way she had trained me to do when I was not allowed to speak but was still required to acknowledge her commands.

Becoming fixated, I signaled for Mother to move more to my left. "Stop." Then after contemplating my new ability, I signaled, "Up. Stop. Turn. Stop."

Just in front of me, Mother looked right through me without blinking or taking a single breath. I wanted her to smile, to show me some semblance of maternal connection, but I somehow knew she would remain in a catatonic state.

Feeling myself growing weak, as if losing my battery life in this world, I asked, "Why? Why are you here? What is it you want from me?"

Mother's response rang in my head. "I am only here because of you."

An infinity of silence followed.

Becoming even more drained, I strained to look up. Without any emotion she elaborated, "I have always been here, or wherever else you called me to be. This," she spread her hands as if she were spreading her wings, "is entirely your creation. This is all you. Has always been all you. It is you who can't let go. It is you who keeps punishing yourself."

I shuddered from the realization that all my nightmares had little to do with my deviant antagonist. They had always been about me and what I *brought* into my own creations.

CHAPTER 17

RECONCILE

"PROBIE!" the captain barked over the PA system, "get your ass down here right now!"

I had screwed up. I'd miscounted the chimes from the electronic bells. After a few times, I should have known better. But I was too engrossed in one of my passions.

With a fork full of steaming, home-cooked gourmet food just a mere bite away, I raised my eyebrows to the other men happily grazing at their lunch. They simultaneously gave me that distinctive preadolescent you-are-in-so-much-trouble stare.

In a second I dropped the fork, and before it clattered on the plate, I sprang up. I decided against sliding down the pole to my right, but instead pivoted left and flew down the short flight of stairs, then sprinted just as the lumbering red truck gained momentum as it raced out from the station. After a quick jump, I grabbed the pole with one hand; with the other, I flipped the silver handle to open the side door. I then easily plopped into my seat as the fire engine made a hard right on San Francisco's Post Street before blaring its horn.

In the front compartment to my right, in the command seat, was the legendary Fernando De Alba, better known as Captain Hondo, in charge of one of the busiest fire stations in the country. He leaned back and smirked, "Damn, Probie!"

I smiled back. "You know it, Captain, but damned in a good way."

In the seat directly in front of me, a slightly younger firefighter who doubled as a paramedic chimed in as he slapped my knee. "Just means more KP time!"

The engine weaved in and out of traffic as if it were an Aston Martin. After tapping on a large tablet-like touch screen, Hondo, on a headset, informed the crew, "Everybody up? We have an adult male… fifty-plus… difficulty breathing. That's it."

On separate headsets the paramedic and EMT acknowledged the captain. After a few seconds of silence, I felt as if everyone were waiting for something else. "1522… you up?"

In an instant, I mashed down on the intercom button, and in order not to clog the airwaves, I kept my response perfectly curt. "Rog, Captain. I'm up."

"Can't be part of the crew if you're not part of the crew."

Bouncing inside the cabin, the men smiled. Everyone knew that I had just been granted the gift of a lifetime. In the back of my pants pocket, as I had with every mission I had flown for the air force, the birth of my son, Stephen, whom I named after my father, and even when I ran with the centennial torch for the Olympic Games, I carried a thick black leather case that held my dad's silver firefighter badge—number 1522.

"Twenty-two copies," I replied.

Hondo leaned over, shaking his head. "Twenty-two's a negative. No such ID."

I nodded. "Roger, *1522* copies."

"That's Probie 1522," the captain corrected. "So, Prob, when we jump out, you stay on me. 'Kay?"

I again pushed the black button. "Copy. Jump out, I'm on you."

"And Probie, one more thing." Hondo paused as a car in front of our engine suddenly veered away at the last second. "Make him proud."

"Always!" I replied.

From nowhere I found my smile—that rarest of ever so buried expressions that had always made me radiate with every fiber of my being. The same beaming, end-to-end smile that I had when I held my newborn son, when Stephen took his first steps in his bare feet on a few blades of spiky grass, and when I chased after him the afternoon he rode his tiny red bike completely by himself.

It was the exact sensation I had felt when I was initially in foster care at the Catanzes' home, when I had finally saved enough money from doing chores to buy parts to fix up my bicycle, and when I finally rode it up and down the steep street, praying for that day to never end—that distinct, thrilling rush that blew across my face—deliverance.

Years later, before each and every flight, as I stepped into my air force flight suit, that quiet sense of belonging and pride had made me walk a little different and stand just a little taller.

Way before my second divorce, through my own actions and choices, by simply trying to keep up with everything I had squandered untold happiness. I was always appreciative, but ever so slowly, I'd developed a defensive habit of becoming fearful of what may be around the next corner.

I realized how disconnected I had become when once, after I returned from the road, Marsha and our four staff members went out of their way to celebrate that after more than two hundred weeks on the *New York Times* best-seller list, *A Child Called "It"* finally captured the number one slot. After receiving a few cheers and seeing the banner and elaborate cake, I quickly and nervously thanked everyone before fleeing into the sanctuary of my office so I could instead get a handle on the stacks of paperwork.

And yet, with one simple gesture, like when I had first met Hondo and he had flung me his firefighter's protective bunker jacket—"Just in case we get a serious call," he'd said with a smile—I had grinned from ear to ear. I was only at the station for an hour, but I clung on to that jacket like a preschool child who refused to let go of his favorite blanket.

I had felt the same sense of joy and camaraderie when I was fifteen and living with the Turnbough family. One Sunday afternoon, during a rare visit with Father in the big city, I met him at a different fire station because his, Station 3, was closed for renovation. The shift captain took me for a ride in the front section of the engine. Dressed in an oversized turnout coat and wearing a leather fireman's helmet, those few minutes in the cab—tugging on the chain that activated the siren, turning behind me to gaze at my father and the other men around him—somehow silenced my anxieties. I was safe, and I was accepted.

Once again bouncing around inside the engine's rear cab like a loose item in a bag of groceries, still beaming from within, I realized just how brutal the last few years had been. I took on so much because I still didn't feel safe enough to let down my guard and therefore didn't allow true happiness to seep in.

Suddenly the engine lurched to a stop. In a flash, all of us leapt out. As I circled my way around to the front of the bright red fire engine, I saw the two medics snatch up additional gear.

"Probie," the captain said as he pointed toward an open bay of the truck, "grab the defibrillator."

I gave a quick nod before grabbing the machine by the handle and ran to catch up with the three other men. As the four of us rushed through the lobby, a horde of people stepped aside. After standing in front of the elevator for more than a minute, I gestured to Hondo that a stairwell was just to our left. With a quick nod, the captain gave me permission. I rocketed up the stairs. Less than two flights later, I lost all my energy. I heard Captain Hondo just behind me, and I caught a glimpse of the two medics breezing past me, taking two steps at a time.

As the captain began to overtake me, I huffed, "How many more flights?"

"Just four more. Come on, Probie."

I couldn't believe, I couldn't accept, that *this* was happening to *me.* With all that had swirled around my crazy life, I had always remained in pretty good shape. "But then again," my oxygen-starved mind rang out, "you are..."

"Probie," the captain barked as I reached the hallway of the sixth floor, "the machine."

After passing the defibrillator to the EMT, I bent down as if the act itself would somehow provide me with more air. As I did, one of the medics looked at me with his hand on an oxygen mask, gesturing toward me.

I playfully waved him off, but as an ambulance crew arrived to put the disabled gentleman on a stretcher, it hit home when someone announced the man's age: fifty-one.

I became completely incensed at myself. Even though I still went to the gym to jog out a couple of miles on the treadmill, and put in some time with the weights, I really wasn't working out like *me*, the dig-deep-down intense part of me, I realized as I helped to guide the gurney down the narrow hallway.

I had sensed a drastic change in myself when I returned after spending nearly a month in the immediate aftermath of Katrina. I was proud to play a small part in another disaster recovery effort, although I was devastated and even ashamed that so much went so wrong. Like many others, I felt that more could have been done *directly* for those who lost everything and were desperate for the smallest crumb of assistance. When I returned to the safety of my spacious home a few days before leaving for a national book tour, I had found myself suddenly bawling, whether just sitting having a cup of coffee or watching some stupid television commercial. After checking in with a friend who also had challenges adjusting to life after Katrina, I discovered I had (or had had for several decades) survivor's guilt.

My next major decline had come upon me through a series of events when I returned home from my second trip to Iraq. My right hand started shaking uncontrollably. I was overwhelmed with fatigue, as if the last forty-plus years of my hypersonic odyssey had suddenly run out of fuel and crashed. So, instead of sweating at the gym and toning my body, expanding my mind through my college assignments, or even working on my latest writing project, I simply sat outside seemingly for hours without blinking, reading books in just over a day or covering myself as if I were in my own private cocoon when taking long naps.

Part of it was I just *never* wanted to come remotely close to even thinking about growing old. As much as I had microplanned far-flung goals, and completed multi-level tasks with considerable ease, I never gave too much thought to my senior years. And I certainly didn't want to entertain the cold, hard fact that with all my oddities, and failing twice at the sacred vows, that I might never find a person that I wouldn't have to save, fix, or constantly prove my worth to.

Discovering my mortality on the staircase, from inside my head, a line from my past screamed, "How many more summers do I have left?"

Later that afternoon, after cleaning the fire station and washing the engine, I stood alone outside with my back against the redbrick wall. Even though I wore a T-shirt and thick purple San Francisco Fire Department sweat-shirt, the January day made me shiver all the same. Like my father before me, I indulged in my vice. But rather than a cigarette, I smoked a short cigar, thinking of my father and the devotion he'd had with his brothers at Station 3.

After years of my quest to discover anything remotely personal about my father, it was literally a few feet from where I stood that I unexpectedly found some answers. Last year, when I first met Hondo face-to-face, a gentleman from the past appeared with a warm smile and a big hug—Al Gughemetti, a man I had met at my father's funeral service.

Meeting Al at the fire station with his wife, Doris, by his side, it was as if the three of us were a heartbeat away from tears. During what began as an awkward moment that stretched into several seconds, I kept my head down. I did so by habit—in shame of the past: mine, my father's, and that of The Family.

After a few salutations, I dived in: "Is there anything… that… you can tell me? What was my dad like?"

Mr. Gughemetti laid the foundation that Father and his best friend, Lee "Tiger" Lane (whom my two brothers and I called Uncle), Andy Bronzich, and Al had worked together for years, twenty-four hours on, forty-eight hours off, on B watch.

"Back in the day," Al reminisced, "we'd get a call, roll out, and like kids, closer we got to the fire, the more amped up everyone got."

"No way, my dad excited? Wow!"

"Now, you got to understand, back then, we didn't have any safety equipment—no mask, Scott packs*, nothing, just your brothers beside you and a set of balls. Anyway, your dad was first in, last out."

"No way!" The impressionable little boy inside me yipped with glee.

* An oxygen canister attached to a face mask.

"So what's the first thing Tiger, Brons, and your old man do when they finish a job? Stand around in a circle, passing around a lighter to have a smoke! Coughing, spitting, sometimes puking from eating all that crud, but nothing could keep 'em too far from each other." Mr. Gughemetti stopped, as if teaching me a lesson. "Can't put it into words.""

"Camaraderie," I replied. I had felt that samc sense of trust with Tim Johnson while traveling throughout Southern Louisiana in the aftermath of Katrina, and with my flight crew when I flew in the air force.

"I tell you, with your dad," Al said with a laugh, "I loved to pull his chain. He always insisted on setting the table. Every utensil had to be precisely placed—forks, knives, serving spoons, you name it."

I recalled when Father held my preschool wrist as he instructed me how to set the table. I remembered craning my head up as far as possible, beaming with pride as I placed everything in its proper setting to make Father proud.

"So, the moment Stevie turns around, I'd come behind him and move everything, every which way. Drove him crazy, completely nuts. He'd hit the roof. Every shift, every meal, same thing, he'd yell, 'Where's that Dago son of a bitch!' Always got a laugh. Never failed."

"No way!" I shouted. "My dad used that type of language?" I laughed along with Doris.

"Hell, we all did. We were brothers. That's why..." He suddenly stopped dead to look at his wife, who nodded as if giving Al permission. "None of us knew for years what was going on. Your dad taking all those extras, covering so many shifts, after a while we knew there was trouble at home, but we never imagined how bad it was."

Again I bent my head down, fighting not to flee or burst into tears from the Hoover Dam—sized wall of shame that I still held inside.

"David, believe me, we did try to help your father," Doris spoke up.

Al coughed, as if to interject. "So, ah, one day, I drive Stevie home, and as we got close, you could cut the tension with a knife. Anyway, we get to Crestline, and he asks, 'Can you wait a minute?' So I wait, and I'll never forget this, and a few minutes later he comes back with that beat-up blue Pan American bag of his, and he's crying.

"The only thing he says is, 'She won't let me in.'"

He then stopped as if to recover from his own pain. "So, I take him to our place, Doris makes sure he has something to eat, and we drove him back to the station so at least he could bunk out and have a place to sleep. That's before your mom kicked him out in January and he moved to Eddy Street*. Again, we just didn't know. We should've done more." Al nodded to his wife, who returned the gesture toward me.

Doris reached out to hold my hand. "David, you have to understand, your mother, she was so cruel."

Wanting to tear the skin off my body from disgust, I blurted out, "*She* was a bitch." Upon hearing my own proclamation, I covered my mouth. As I tried to apologize for my bad language in front of my father's lifetime friends, they both laughed with approval.

* A dingy "motel row" area of the city. By coincidence, during a call that day at the firehouse, Captain Hondo pointed out the exact motel where my father had stayed before he was admitted to Kaiser Hospital, where he died of cancer.

"Anyway," Al finished, "it's important for you to know, for your brothers to know, that we did try to help."

With every word, I wanted to scream to God Almighty, "How in the world can so many people—my teachers, families I had met from the old neighborhood, those at the fire station, and Lord knows who else—carry so much guilt because of *her*? How is it that so many people suffered because of one person's absolute hate? *Why?*"

Yet instead of expelling my own wrath, with the purest sincerity, I stated, "I can't—I mean, my brothers and I can never thank you both enough for being there for my dad. I just can't begin to tell you how much as a kid, especially when I was in foster care, how much I used to cry inside when I worried about my dad being alone and hungry."

As I stupidly rambled away, clutching Hondo's bunker jacket, I could feel my excitement being replaced by fatigue from being overly exposed to Mother.

"David," Al gently said, "like I said, at the station, we were all brothers."

I thought of my own siblings and all those summers that had slipped away.

Before I could journey down that path, Mr. Gughemetti added, "That's why I went to the park to help your dad out."

Suddenly, I felt flushed. My face became taut and I knew if I didn't switch off in the next second, I would indeed lose it. Of all the experiences between Mother and me, our time at the park…

"That was you?" I practically whispered, choking up, craving the thread of an answer to the question that had haunted me for years, exactly how my magical moment with my mother had come to be. "The park, sir, you said the park?"

"Why, yes," Al said with a chuckle. "Memorial Park."

My brain screamed as if I had shoved my entire arm into an electrical outlet.

"I think it was your family's first trip there. Steve used to take you all to, ah, nearby Portola Park. Anyway, I guess on the way down, that ole Chevy of yours..."

"The station wagon," I interrupted.

"Yep, you know the one. Well, it broke down."

"The radiator?" I pried.

"I think so, now that you mention it. Well, next day, your dad calls the station, an' the captain gives me a release so I drove down the coast, picked up your dad, and your brother...?"

"Ron! Dad and you took Ronald." I remembered how Ron, Stan, and I had always vied for any private moment with Father and how that morning, at the campsite, Ron and Stan had fought to be the one chosen to join Father and Al. Because of my status, I didn't dare to even think of making the slightest effort.

"Nice boy, had your father's eyes and hair. So anyway, everybody knew before I became a firefighter, I used to work at the airport for United Airlines, and before that, for the air force, fixin' B-47s back in the day, so it was no big deal, nothing really," Al proudly stated.

Hearing the words, connecting how everything fit together, I felt my blood rush. I thanked God for the blessing of allowing me to discover how my most precious moment with my mother came to be, sitting on the far end of a fallen tree, my feet happily dangling over a small summer creek. While I used both hands to clutch a flimsy, bright red plastic fishing pole, I felt the gentle but firm tug of Mother's grip on my belt. I couldn't believe my luck. Even as I dared to rest the upper part of my back against Mother's chest, Mom didn't flinch. If anything, Mother seemed to scoot closer toward me.

Below us, Stan angrily kicked the pebbles and rocks while shouting for Mother's attention, as if she had obviously chosen the wrong child, and I stole a mere whiff of her perfume. And that's when Mother leaned even closer and whispered the three most important words of my life: "It's our time."

Those few minutes at the park seemed to wash all sins and humiliation completely away.

Resting against the cold brick wall of the fire station, the memory still made me beam. Back then there were countless times when I didn't think I'd crawl away from Mother's sinister torture, let alone make it out alive. And now, just days after passing the midcentury mark, I knew that because of my past, I would have to do many things differently. I'd never thought I'd make it this far.

"But now," I adamantly told myself, "you've got to be better. Live better. Take more responsibility for your actions and your inactions. Choose more wisely. Lessen your exposure to anything and anyone that's toxic, and reclaim your sense of worth. And for God's sake, stop chasing after everyone's approval and let go of your shame. You've got to let go of her."

Later that evening, after sharing another gourmet meal at the fire station, I thanked all the men for the experience and then piloted my SUV south of San Francisco to my childhood town of Daly City. Stopping in front of the house on Crestline Avenue, as always, I gave a quick prayer for my brothers, but this time I added both Mother and Father to my private devotion.

As the fog began to thicken around my vehicle, I dared myself to take another journey into my past by driving the same coastal route as Mother had when she had taken Ron, Stan, Russell, and me to the once-cherished state park.

With my heater on and my moonroof wide open, I took in the distinctive fragrance of the eucalyptus trees. As I approached the southern end of the city, I smiled at a local relic, the Sea Bowl bowling alley, which had so captivated my brothers and me. It was then that I realized that I should focus on making everything less arduous and more enjoyable.

As I approached Devil's Slide, infamous for its steep, eroded slopes and massive rock slides, like Mother before me, I maintained a death grip on the steering wheel while carefully scanning the mist-filled twisty roads for any debris. As I did, I couldn't help but recall as a small child how Ron, Stan, and I would ever so carefully scoot over to the right side of the clunky station wagon and peek through the window. Then, seeing nothing but the jagged edges of the cliff and the ocean's foaming water far below, whenever the tires squealed, out of fright, the three of us grabbed each other's arms for support.

Arriving at the fancy hotel in Half Moon Bay, I grabbed my bag and entered the prestigious lobby, which bustled with well-dressed couples leaving after their dinners. As always, I obviously looked out of place, but this time I didn't care.

After washing the grime from my face, I stood outside my ground-level room by a small lit firepit beside a pair of worn wooden chairs. Enjoying a glass of red wine, along with the hypnotic slapping sound of the hurtling waves just a few feet away, I was tired yet completely rested.

At the fire station, I had begun to feel a quiet sense of knowing that, with all that I'd learned, all that I had done, and all that I had been blessed with, there was still much more to discover. I *still* had much more work to do on myself to become a better, more whole person. With my acceptance, I could actually feel my fear and some of the lifelong shame slowly dissipate.

As I became surrounded by the swirling, fog-filled droplets, I knew I didn't have all the time in the world—I never did—but I had all the time I needed to put my life in order for the remainder of my years.

I was ready.

That evening in my dream, I found myself in darkness. In my head, I could hear the gentle yet building distinctive notes of a song from a movie about a man who, also haunted by his past, uses his dream world to try to somehow rectify the reality of his actual one.

Then I saw it. Perfectly. It was so clear, so brilliant, I could smell the fragrance of the setting and absorbed all its purity. But then, I'd always had that blessing.

As always, with deep intensity, I focused to keep my mind still so I didn't venture somewhere else.

Mother was regal and adoring, as only mothers can be, and I saw the elementary-school version of my endless smile. I stood far enough away out of respect for the dignity of the moment, but also so as not to ruin this marvel.

"Beautiful," I announced.

"Yes," Mother agreed as she appeared beside me, "it was."

I caught the nuance.

She's right.

As the music being played inside my head built, I also picked up the soothing, echoing sounds from the stream. I began to sense a deep revelation. As I did, Mother leaned over. "Yes."

I swallowed hard, taking my eyes off the fantasy of Mother. In the next moment, I bent over with my fingers running through the cold liquid. "Water," I proclaimed. "My solace has always been water." I stopped myself as I looked up at the giggling boy staring down at me with his baited hook jerking just above the stream, as if he had always known something I had just discovered.

As I unsteadily stood up, I saw a series of kaleidoscopic flashes: Mother driving the car through Golden Gate Park, slowing down at the thundering Rainbow Falls; how I clung to the brass seahorse-shaped barrier to catch a glimpse of the ancient Steinhart Aquarium's famed swamp filled with alligators and swarms of red-eared turtles; skipping stones on the Russian River with my father and then teaching my son to do it at the same spot; a photo of myself midair, refueling the SR-71 Blackbird over Idaho's green-blue Salmon River; even my yearning to have my own koi pond. It was water that always brought me a cleansing sense of tranquility.

"Water," I said again, but with more conviction. "It fed me when you wouldn't. It helped to heal me after I was stabbed by you. It made me feel clean whenever I felt dirty. It's always been my resource."

"Yes," Mother politely stated inside my head.

I could feel myself begin to shudder. A deep, tightening band around my chest began to take hold. I could feel myself slipping away, and above all, beyond anything, real world or not, I craved for *this* not to slip away. Without thinking, like a small, panic-stricken child, I instinctively reached out and snatched my mother's hand.

In a blink, I was in the exact same spot, but the setting itself was different. There was no gleeful mother and son. No fishing pole. No warm sensation from the sun's rays. Instead, the weather was suddenly gray and cold, the air filled with light rain, and the mighty log was much smaller, worn and decayed.

Beside me, I could feel Mother waiting for me to tell her of my quest.

"I stayed away for years. No one knew, not a soul.

"So, there was this lady who worked at juvenile probation at Hillcrest, and she had read the books about my time in foster care and wanted me to come out and speak to the kids."

Mother nodded for me to go on.

"For years I turned her down. It was too close to the bone and I was too ashamed of when I was in Hillcrest, especially when you tried to convince Dad, Gram, the boys, social services, and everyone else who'd listen that you had to *discipline* me because I was some possessed arsonist who was hell-bent on burning down the world. You knew that would poison Dad. It was like you could destroy two lives with one lie. Then, you fought to have me put away in a mental institution, as if being removed from The Family weren't enough.

"Anyway," I went on, "I finally agreed. So, of course, I'm on the road, and that Friday morning, I'm in Salt Lake City doing volunteer work at a big fund-raiser for a friend, and I lose my voice. It's completely gone. I could actually feel the cords inside my throat stretch like they were going to snap. It was like breathing through a straw. The more I fought to breathe, the tighter everything got. I felt myself turn blue in front of everyone."

I stopped for a moment, wanting to keep Mother out of my head.

"Did you even have the faintest idea of what you've done? You made me swallow ammonia, not once, but twice. The second time was right in front of Dad. And he… he just stood there as I fell to his shoes.

"My God, why do I chase *you*?"

I gazed up at the log, flushing away whatever anger had begun to build. "This is not about that," I told myself.

"Between the ammonia thing from years ago, all the traveling, all the speaking, with no rest, I knew one day it *might* be a possibility. I knew that one day, the day may come, I just… told myself, if I didn't address it—my past, *our* past—maybe it wouldn't have an effect on me." I exhaled deeply, trying not to stray too far.

"Afterwards, I'm at the airport. I'm so drained, I got nothing left, I just want to crawl into a bed and hide, but there's delay after delay after delay. I can't eat because I'm too afraid I might suddenly throw up, in public, again. Finally, five, six hours later, I land in San Fran and I'm so excited, nothing bothers me. Even when I can't find my directions to Half Moon Bay, I don't care." I felt myself becoming flushed with excitement. "Somehow I knew what road to take. I'll never forget driving through the Crystal Springs Reservoir, then down Highway 92 to the coast, the windy curves, the smell of the trees bathed in fog, it reminded me of…"

"Christmastime," Mother answered inside my head.

"Yeah, Christmas with The Family. So, I check into this amazing hotel that's decorated from head to toe with holiday decorations everywhere. I get this tiny room that faces the ocean. The first thing I do is fling open the curtains and, even though it's raining, I open the window. You used to take us all to Half Moon Bay for pumpkins before Halloween, and I just thought being there again might bring me closer to…"

This time Mother didn't finish my rambling sentence.

"The next day I spent at Hillcrest juvenile hall, then I drove an hour away to this boot camp, which was, I didn't know was…"

"A few miles away from the park," Mother finished.

"I really didn't even think about it. I just followed the lady in my rental, and when we made the turn to the juvenile boot camp, I knew then that the park was…"

"Just a few miles away," Mother said with her tone more adamant.

I fought to keep my cool. "Later that Saturday night, I can't sleep. My throat's killing me, I'm exhausted, but at the same time, I'm amped. 'The park,' it rings constantly inside my head."

I stopped to emphasize my point. "Here's the thing, the next day, I have it off, I don't have to fly anywhere, do anything, and that *never* happens. So I buy one of those cheap Instamatic pocket cameras and I'm on my way. You have no idea!" I excitedly proclaimed. "I never go out, venture anywhere for myself. I like to stay put, it's a safety-exposure boundary thing," I confessed with my voice trailing off.

"Yes," Mother agreed. "I know."

"I take the same coastal highway, just like you did, then turn left, seeing those same worn, red barns. I find the road that turns steep up and to the right. An' even though the sign says a few miles, it takes forever. The closer I get, the more nervous I become. I want to bail. I feel that maybe I passed it, the weather's getting too bad, any excuse I can make..."

I stopped, feeling the pressure in my chest return. "Then, right before I stop and turn around, I find it. That wooden sign with bright yellow paint."

"Memorial Park," Mother stated. I could feel her begin to connect to my childhood wonder.

"I can't explain it. Even though I'm driving, it's like I'm eight, nine again, when I first saw everything. Everything is the same, the wooden ranger station on your left, the pathway of trees, the old snack shack, everything! And the best part, I'm the only one there. I step out of the SUV, and it's so cold you could see your breath. It's like being Lewis and Clark, you're the only one seeing something that's so pristine for the very first time."

"Heaven," Mother sighed.

At that moment, I actually felt *her* pain.

In the real world, I recalled studying the collage of photos of Mom and Dad fishing, Mom in the snow, Mom chopping wood—Mom, as a person, being one with nature. Rarely did I think of Mother's own connection with the outdoors.

"So, I quietly close the door to the SUV, careful so as not to disturb anything. It's like I'm in a dream. But I know I'm not dreaming. The place is so quiet, all I can hear is the random beats of water drops from the trees after the weekend's storms. Then, as if I'm on the surface of the moon, I slowly, carefully, apply pressure with my steps. But everything is so slippery, the blanket of leaves, the twig-sized branches, even the rare patches of dirt.

"Then I remember the outside amphitheater, and that the log is somewhere near that area. It takes me an hour, zigzagging through the park, and duh, I find it right next to where I parked. I get nervous, because I know I'm so close. I go down this worn dirt path, looking over my right shoulder at the small river, stopping every two, three feet, peering through the ferns, trees, everything, trying to find the spot, but it's gone."

"And, was it?" Mother inquired in the same manner that all parents do when they know the answer.

I nearly erupted. "*You* have to understand how much that meant to me, being that close to Daly City, working at Hillcrest the day before, driving to the park, never, ever having any time off, the years of sitting alone in the basement, fantasizing about it. And to end up with nothing. Not a damn thing. It wasn't fair!"

"My little, little David-boy," Mother almost cooed, "at times you are such a child. You should know that life is never fair. It's only what you make of it." She nodded in a parental fashion. "Now, go on, tell me, what happened next?"

I felt a warm surge. I looked at her and like a great archeologist, I beamed. I smiled, just like I had in the real world just a few hours ago at the fire station.

"Yes. My son, you found it. You did it!"

"There were these two redwood trees, like they were placed on the pathway from years ago, and I remembered having to climb up and over them. Why did you let me do that?" I laughed at my own question as if I were simply having a conversation with any other typical person. "I mean, you never let Ron, Stan, or me step one inch off the front lawn when we were kids, we had to check in with you every few minutes so you knew no one snatched us away, we had to sit ten feet away from the TV so it wouldn't fry our eyes out, and that April, the anniversary of the Great Earth Quake, you kept the three of us home from school. You were such a control freak.

"So what were you thinking? Why did you pick me over Stan that day? Why me?"

From behind me, Mother placed her hands gently on my shoulders. I could feel her lean into me. I could feel the gentle pressure of her body rest against mine. I could sense the words about to come out, but selfishly, I had to hear them. "David, David, David," Mother whispered into my ear, just as she had on that beautiful summer morning. "That was our time."

Looking up at the log, I cried inside. I wanted to let it all out, to relieve myself of the years of so much pain, but I couldn't do it. I wouldn't allow myself. I fought to suppress my tears. "Anyway, ah, I find it, the log, and it's nothing like before. It still sticks out over the water, but it doesn't have that dark redwood bark on it, and its stump end is no longer a neat circle like when it was first cut down. It's all gray and smoothed from the years of exposure, like it's tired… but it's still 'the log.'

"I try to take a few pictures, but I can't get it into the frame. There's too much stuff in the way, the angles are wrong, it's too dark, everything's against me. And I'm losing it, like after everything, if I can't get a stupid picture, I'm lost!"

Reliving my experiences through my dream, with Mother standing beside me, was too much. Too much exposure and way too much pain. "You're so close," I informed myself from the deep recesses of my mind. "She's not a threat. Just let it happen. You deserve to free yourself."

I took another breath, stood a little taller.

"I figure if I can find a way to the other side, I can get the shot. So I run from the path, out from the amphitheater and follow the road from the picnic area to the one that leads down past the covered river and then up that steep hill to the campsites. So, after jogging forever, I find it. I find your favorite campsite: B-17!" I remembered how Mother liked this campsite in part because it was a more expansive site that had two large benches with tables, and also because it pleased Ron, who held a fascination with WWII aircraft, the B-17 being one of his favorites.

"Then, without thinking, I find that small trail we all took when you'd take us fishing. But about a half mile into it, it's completely blocked, and I have to double back and find another way, from the opposite side of the park. Time's running out, it's beginning to sprinkle, and I'm getting anxious, so I run full-out, *Marathon Man*, *Running Man*, the whole thing. Then," I exhaled as I could somehow feel the sensation, "everything's so dark and my glasses are so completely fogged up that I run off the side of a hill. Again, full speed, totally airborne.

"All I could remember was opening my eyes and having the sensation as if someone were sitting on my sides. I know I'm not wearing my glasses, but I get frantic when I can't find the camera. With my fingers, I search the area before I stand up so as not to step on my specs, and then when I do, I can't find my keys. But all I think about is the damn Kodak.

"Thank God, I find everything, but now I'm turned around. I have no idea where I'm at, and from above the redwoods I can hear the rain come down. Now, I'm really getting concerned. But," I stopped and turned toward Mother, "I remembered when you were Ron's and my Cub Scout den mother, you used to have us close our eyes and listen for the sounds of water, then follow it, to always keep the sun on one shoulder, so you always knew what direction you where heading. Understand, I've been through weeks and weeks of survival school training with the air force, but all I remembered was everything you had taught me…"

"Here, at this park," Mother said.

"I'm caked with dirt, mud, leaves, you name it. And, I'm soaked to the bone. But I'm so jazzed 'cause I can hear it from a distance, the water. I know I should be careful, that I've already screwed up and how damn lucky I was that I didn't twist an ankle, that I need to get out of there, but I can't, I won't. I follow the sound and sprint towards it. I slip, I slide, on my hands and heels. I'm all over the place, but every time I fall down, I know it's gonna be fine. Without a doubt I am going to find it.

"I come to another drop-off and below me are all these rocks. I jump down, and when my eyes adjust I know exactly where I am. I try to clean my glasses with my T-shirt but they only become more smeared.

"I feel like Tuco from the spaghetti western movie, when he finally finds the gravesite where somewhere his treasure lies. But there's so many of them—hundreds, thousands—that he becomes so overwhelmed, his head begins to spin. Slowly at first, but it quickly picks up until everything becomes a blur. As it does, the music from the film builds until Tuco nearly faints."

"Where were you when you found it?" Mother asked, again knowing the answer.

I swallowed hard. "Exactly where we're standing. And this," I proudly proclaimed, pointing my left arm, "is how I first saw it."

I could feel my heart racing. I also could feel the battery life to my dream world was rapidly draining.

"So," Mother picked up, "you took your pictures and it took you a few hours to find your way out of the park. You must have been quite a sight when you got back to your hotel."

"You should have seen it. There was this huge Christmas party, everyone dressed to the nines, and I limp in. Everyone scrams out of the way like I'm the plague. I find the hotel bar, plop myself down, place the camera on the counter, and order their best glass of Pinot Noir and a clean bar rag to wipe my face."

Simultaneously, Mother and I laughed. "I wish," I began to say.

"But I do," Mother said. "I see it now, just as you did. I know, David, I know."

"Then," I said as I could feel my right hand began to shake, "you know I came to the park for you."

"No," Mother said in the most gentle of tones as she appeared right in front of me. "That's not entirely true. You know that, and you've always known that you came for us."

I bent my head down, as I had a gazillion times before, but this time it had nothing to do with one of her hateful commands. I knew she was right—that my mother was absolutely correct.

"David, I can hear you," Mother said in a playful but firm tone. "You need to say the words. Just say them."

The edges around my world began to change. I slowly looked up. As I did, Mother's head was tilted to one side. She nodded, as if giving me permission. "It's going to be fine."

I flashed a false smile. "Free yourself," the vault from within me whispered.

"You're right." I sighed. "I did. I came for us."

Floating like an angel, Mother turned slightly and extended her right arm. As she did, everything changed. The chilling temperature disappeared, the sky above turned bright blue. I felt the warm rays of the sun on my back. Directly in front of me, where I had actually stood years ago, muddied and bruised, I could see them both: mother and child, sitting happily on the pristine redwood log.

My eyes began to blink uncontrollably. I turned to avoid the sun, but I realized it had nothing to do with its rays. Without reasoning, I blurted, "The thing that killed me the most," I used my fingers to stab my chest, "was I loved you so. That I tried so hard to be that perfect child, to do anything, everything, every day to not piss you off!" I stopped for a moment as I felt myself slip further away. "Even in the basement, after I did all those chores, without any food, at night when everyone was in bed, a real one, I used to pray so hard for you to come back to me that I'd fall asleep on the shitty army cot with my hands clasped together!"

Mother's feet touched the ground. I could hear the crunching sounds as she slowly stepped closer to me, stopping an arm's length in front of me. The last thing I wanted was for her to reach out and touch me. "I know," she stated. "David, I know."

"The hell you do," I lashed. "If anything, Roerva Catherine Christensen-Pelzer, I know you. I know how you were treated, how you were raised, how Gram controlled you and Uncle Dan, how you couldn't escape Gram even as an adult. Even as I lived in that dungeon like some rodent, even then, I felt sorry, so sorry for *you*!"

As I looked up at my dream world, it violently shook as if I were in the middle of an earthquake. But with every confessional statement, I knew I was making my fantasy realm shake all the more.

"In the end, when you had me stand at the top of the basement stairs and you'd squeeze my throat, the more you'd tighten your grip, the more I felt sorry for you, because at least if you killed me, I'd be free. But for you, there'd be no escape. You were torturing yourself as much as you were trying to kill me."

I stopped, letting the last of the tremors settle while I fought to catch my breath and to somehow rebuild my strength.

"You never had a chance. But I did. I would have given anything to have seen the look on your bloated face that Friday when the police officer called you saying I was free. Free of you!

"You have no idea the damage you caused, the endless pits I had to crawl out of every single day. With everything, I fought so damn hard when everyone else did things so easily. The fact that I'm alive, that I'm not rotting away in some dark hole of some jail cell—" I stopped my rant when I saw, when I felt, the torment from within my Mother's eyes.

As I struggled to clear my airway, my picturesque setting returned to normal.

"You have to know how much I should hate you and anything or anybody associated with you. But at the end of the day, at this very moment, I am forever grateful that you gave me life. That I used to feel you rock me when I was sick as a small boy or that you played Christmas albums for me in July so I could sing to you.

"As God is my witness, I can never thank you enough for picking me that day to be with you, for making that moment in time ours. You have no idea how many times this memory," I pointed upward, "saved my life.

"And that's the gift. I was saved. I was loved by so many. I lost so much because of you, but at the same time, I fought and I gained so much because of you.

"But now, I have to be different, do different, live differently. I don't have," I stopped to show Mother the log, our log, "that many more summers left. I miss you both so much. If you knew my Stephen. He's such a good, good man."

My body shook as I lost the remainder of my strength. I felt the same sensation, the exact fear, as I had when I was forced to swallow ammonia. I knew if I passed out here I would never have this chance again. I clenched my right hand, ordering it not to shake, and then commanded myself to stand.

"I've screwed up so much. I can't live like that anymore, the fear, all the anxiety, choosing poorly, the white-hot rage and resentment. I have this grand life, but on the inside, you're killing, I mean, *I'm letting you kill me.* It's my issue, my side of the street. I need to be cleaner, a better, happier person. I don't want to die alone like..."

With no more tears to shed, I met my mother's gaze. "Out of all the people I've saved, I wish I could have rescued you."

With my right hand, I reached out, stretching my fingers to touch the side of Mother's face. The second I felt her softened skin, the shaking stopped. Mother leaned into my open palm, just as I must have when I was a baby, her baby, and needed to be soothed by a loving gesture. I could feel the tears from her eyes form into a small pool. As I did, I could see above me a cloudless sky. Large droplets fell all around us yet did not strike Mother or me. As if releasing her shame, Mother leaned into my hand all the more. "I always loved my *David*... I just hated myself too much."

"I know, I know." I accepted becoming the parental figure. "It's going to be fine. You're going to be fine. It's all going to be fine."

From within, I murmured a quick prayer: "All-loving, all-forgiving Heavenly Father, please grant me the gift of allowing my mother to be free of all pain, pardoned of all sins, and allow *her* the gift of resting in eternal peace. Forever and ever. Amen!"

I opened my eyes. Mother stood, shoeless, in a full-length white dress. A warm breeze picked up, making the bottom of her dress and the ends of her shiny hair flutter. I caught a whiff of her fragrance as I could feel Mother fade from me.

The more Mother's physical outline dimmed, the more radiant her soul shone. In our last moment, I looked through her and felt a surge of release.

Sitting on the log, I could feel the loving bond between parent and child. With purity of heart, I gave them both a confirming nod. "You deserve."

EPILOGUE

The sound of a horrendous crash startles me from my hypnotic concentration. But it's not from being in the middle of another war zone, or the aftereffects that stemmed from a massive natural disaster. Instead it's Mother Nature's gigantic, teal-colored wave slapping the beach just below me. Seconds later a cyclone of swirling mist passes just above my head. My hands release their grip on the rickety, gray, faded fence. From deep within my heart glows. Caught in the wonder, I confess, "I still can't believe it."

Beside me, absorbing the moment herself, is my beautiful bride, Kay, who echoes my same revelation. Without hesitation, I reach out to take her silky smooth hand. After a few moments and a string of silent prayers, I lead Kay back toward our new dream home, which sits hidden behind a huge fir tree and is just off the coastal pathway. After closing the thick Nana door, I can still hear the relaxing echo from the waves. And, as I do countless times every day, I stare at the panoramic, high-definition view of the ocean blending with the blue sky.

Again I smile. The same smile that I had found when I was at Father's fire station just a few years ago. As of late, that giddy sensation finds me several times a day.

I walk past my piano knowing I need to dedicate more time to learning a new song. After teaching myself to convert a few Pat Metheny ballads, I almost feel confident enough to attempt Sakamoto's "Merry Christmas Mr. Lawrence." Passing a divider, I stop to gaze back outside at the angled corner of the house. I look down at the bright seasonal flowers I planted, a score of neatly arranged, shiny black rocks and a half-dome-shaped piece of wood where my companion of nearly thirty years, my pet box turtle, Chuck, now rests. I feel comforted that his resting place receives the late afternoon sun. And, at his advanced age, I am grateful he was able to make the recent long journey up north to the new home.

My eyes then pick up a visitor from outside. Normally, it's a herd of deer that slowly graze a mere few feet in front of our lounge chairs, but as of late, a fox has decided he has the need to be adopted by sitting, basking, or sleeping on our thick concrete deck.

"Company," I fling out behind me.

Kay's eyes light up. "Is it our Mister Foxx?"

"Who else?" I jest.

Kay immediately ceases whatever she deems important and sprints over to the large set of glass doors. Then, ever so slowly, she carefully opens the door, tiptoes, out and begins to court our guest.

My grin fails to recede. I never thought I could be this relaxed or this happy—every single day.

I am so blessed.

Meeting Kay and slowly getting to know her and then her expansive, supportive family was beyond a Godsend. After a pressing bump in the road (which I caused), I finally quit running, grew up, and seriously prayed about the possibility of a future with her. Out of all the relationships I've been fortunate enough to share in, Kay was the only person who didn't put conditions on her love, have the constant dread of drama following her, or that I didn't feel the overwhelming urge to have to rescue.

After my divorce, and then, after a roller coaster of experiences, both business and personal, I felt the need to finally stop and take the time and genuine effort to work on myself. Part of that process was letting go of my shame, which went hand in hand with my desire to do so much for so many. Another obstacle for me was trying not to get so spun up on the distant future, doing only what I could with each and every single day, and simply enjoying the moment. After working through that, I finally permitted myself to feel a sense of value and that I actually deserved to share my life with someone of Kay's stature.

I look outside and laugh to myself as Kay coos to Mr. Foxx, who just wants to stretch his limbs before taking his afternoon nap.

"Who would have thought…?" I muse.

I've known for years how lucky I've been, and age and experience only brought it home all the more. I've tried to console a foster family that had their newly adopted baby literally sucked from their arms during an F-5 tornado. I've also closed the eyes of a dying woman who, after working twenty-two years scrubbing toilets in a hotel, and just three days prior to retiring, mistakenly stepped off the curb, slammed her head on the street, and died.

Then, I had four important people in life my pass away in four short months. One on Christmas Eve, and another unexpectedly, my beloved elementary school teacher, the vibrant Mrs. Konstan.

In nearly thirty years of my campaign, I have met, consoled, and held hands with hundreds of thousands of individuals who had become utterly destroyed by their pasts. This makes me realize how amazingly lucky I am to be mentally, physically, and spiritually where I am today.

I've changed. I no longer starve myself, nor do I punish myself by working sixteen-plus hours a day, three hundred plus days a year. I will not allow myself to be taken advantage of, for I know my value. I do my best not to stupidly try to prove myself by chasing others' approval. And most of all, I will no longer associate myself with those who are deliberately toxic.

As simpleton as it sounds, I haven't got time for the pain.

At the back nine of my life, seeing Kay outside squatting as she surveys Mr. Foxx, I still can't fathom that I live in such a pristine setting a few miles above my beloved Russian River. I love having that thread of a connection, and my location even makes it easier for me to take in a ball game with my grown son and his wife in The City by the Bay.

In all, throughout my entire life, I stepped up, stepped out, took a few chances, made a lot of mistakes, and yet, looking outside at God's creation, I got lucky.

No person could ask for anything more.

I step outside to be with my wife. As I study Kay and the fox now sunning itself, I notice that inside, in the corner bedroom window, Gato the diva cat is meowing her warning while pawing the glass.

I begin to open my mouth to launch a quick quip when my pager goes off. Without a word, explanation, or thought, I return inside and go into my closet, where I put on my purple multipocket pants and zip up my black boots. I grab my cap and my father's badge and march out.

In the driveway, to save time, my SUV is faced nose-out. As I concentrate on my pager again, I flip open the back hatch to check my gear. I have my mask with glass inserts, my boots pulled into turnout pants, and my jacket that I still call a "bunker jacket." Inside my apparel, I carry more equipment than should be humanly allowed: four different sets of seven separate flashlights, car battery cable cutters, twenty-five-foot web gear, a pull-drag line, duct tape, a window punch-out device, medical scissors that can practically cut through Kevlar, an all-in-one tool, extrication gloves, medical gloves, and a thick leather belt with an attached metal ring that can help me carry an axe while scurrying up a ladder.

Personally, my most prized piece of equipment is my helmet. With a simple explanation my captain, Shelley Spear, allowed me to create my badge number. Years before the birth of my beloved son, Stephen, out of sense of belonging, I carried my father's badge: 1522. And now I have my own: 1522-A.

After a quick inventory, I slam the hatch shut. With every part of my being, I focus on the stream of information from my response call. But my world instantly stops when I hear the sweet sound of Kay's voice. I tip my cap and bow to her.

"Be careful now, Probie," she jests with a seductive wink. "You come back now, you hear!"

I can't pass up the childlike opportunity. In my best deadpan Schwarzenegger voice, I quip, "I'll be back." Then, stealing another moment, I bore straight into her eyes and confess, "I'll be back, for you, you saucy little minx."

With the setting sun and laced blue-orange sky behind me, I race off, living out another of my life's adventures.

PERSPECTIVES

PATSY

My name is Patsy*. I am Dave's first wife and the mother of his son, Stephen. I have known Dave since about 1985. When I first noticed him he was wearing an air force flight suit and was coming and going in the apartment complex where we both lived. I playfully followed him for the longest time. His apartment was next to mine. About a month later, I think I was the first to say "hello" because I wanted to meet him and check out what kind of person he was.

Dave was different from the other men I knew because he had a job, and I was fascinated by his looks and his posture. He carried himself so well. There was something about him, and I really liked to look at him in his green air force flight suit.

When I became pregnant with Dave's child, I was scared and couldn't believe it. It became a weird situation when his foster mother and my mother got involved. Dave's foster mother, Alice, told Dave to do the right thing and marry me.

* Name has been changed.

Dave was a good provider, but it was hard living on air force pay. And because Dave was on duty so much, I was a stay-at-home mother. Dave was a great father when he was home, but he was gone so much with the air force. We would take spur-of-the-moment camping trips when he got time off, to Guerneville or other places.

When Stephen was about ten months old, Dave wanted to show him off to his mother and brothers. Dave's mother's house was dirty, and she smelled like alcohol and had greasy hair. She barely looked at Stephen, and I couldn't wait to get my baby out of that house because of the conditions. It was a weird event.

Dave and I have remained friends over the years. He has helped me financially, mentally, and spiritually. I can talk to him about anything. I trust him as my friend and I will always love him.

In my opinion, Marsha, Dave's second wife, was not good for him. She got him to move away from his son, Stephen. She had to be the center of attention, and I tried not to have conversations with her. She never loved the real Dave, just the Dave she wanted him to be—which always involved money.

In his thirty-year mission to save children and make a difference in the world, Dave has sacrificed marriage, family, and home time. He will always sacrifice something to save that one child.

Dave is a very loving and caring person who will always be my friend no matter what. It is about friendship. What you see is the real person. He is not BS—it is the real Dave.

MARY MEARSE

My name is Mary Mearse, and I think of Dave as my brother. It never enters my mind about him being a foster brother. I have known Dave since he was thirteen years old. My first memory of him is at a family gathering of Dad's side of the family in a rented hall for Thanksgiving. David was everywhere, looking to see what was happening. He didn't want to miss a moment of the celebration.

My parents raised foster children the whole time I was growing up. Then about the time I was sixteen we moved and my parents took a break from fostering. Then after I married, my parents again opened their home to foster girls, and David came along about that time. He was the first boy in their household. At that time, about the only time I saw David was at family holidays. The other, older teenage foster girls hung out together and had families in thc area they visited, but I do not remember David visiting his family.

It was obvious to me observing David that he worked at a very young age and worked hard. My perception was he wanted to make something of himself and had his agenda. He was eager to learn and to do things.

The first real connection I had with David was when he was in the air force and my parents were having a difficult time. David took military leave and rode his motorcycle all the way from Florida to California, where we met and worked together to try to help them work through their problems. The next step in my relationship with David was when he was divorced from Patsy and Marsha was editing his book. He would call and talk to me about relationships, and I began to see a more mature David. That brought about the bother/sister feeling for me. After my dad died, David would call regularly, and this kept the connection growing. Then one time when David came to visit, we went to Starbucks. This was not only my first time ever at a Starbucks; it was also the first time we got into deep conversations about life. David even talked about wanting to do a book signing at a Barnes and Noble someday in the future.

Well, that future came for David on a day in February in 2004. My husband and I attended David's book signing for *A Child Called "It"* at the Barnes and Noble in Fresno, CA. We were taken aback because years earlier we had attended various signings, and while the turnouts were usually good, they were nothing like this one. Everything had taken a 360-degree turn and we were on cloud nine. It was clear how much everyone loved David. I will never forget that day.

I am so very proud of all of Dave's accomplishments. He has done wonderfully and it is a privilege to be part of his life. I talk about him all the time and ask people if they have read his books. I still remember the first time I read his first three books (*A Child Called "It," The*

Lost Boy, and *A Man Named Dave*). It was on a weekend horse riding trip with my husband. I don't ride, so I purposely brought David's books to read. I read all three in one weekend.

I think of David as very determined, very honest, and trustworthy. It is part of his character. He is the only person besides my husband who tells me the truth: not what I need to hear, but the truth. He is a calming force. Who would think, knowing David as he was at age twelve, that this would happen? He has been my saving grace, and I love and appreciate him. He will always be my brother.

STAN

My name is Stan[*] and I am David's younger brother. I am 52 years old.[**]

When I was very little, about seven years old, I began to notice that my bother David was being picked on by Mother more than my other brothers. I remember always asking Mother if David could come out of the corner to play with me. David was my friend and brother and I worried about him being in the corner. I remember always playing with David at school during recess. We played Frisbee. At home David was never able to play with me because he had too many chores.

At first I didn't realize what the mother I loved so much was doing to my brother. Slowly over time, day by day, I became sad and confused and wondered why Mother was doing things to David.

I don't remember David being taken away from school on his "rescue day," but I do think I remember being told by Mother that David tried to burn the school down and that is why he was taken away.

[*] Name has been changed.

[**] Stan has Bell's palsy.

When everyone was reading his book, I don't have clear memories about saying things in the past against David. There was so much drama surrounding everything and I got pressured to say things. It felt like a carjack.

David has helped me and my family and been supportive and has helped me financially as much as he can. We talk sometimes on Sundays; I tell him about the weather and then we talk about our sons.

It is awesome David has been involved with the child abuse and awareness cause for the last twenty-five years. I think he is doing a fantastic and outstanding job. He is dedicated to his work and helping children. I would like to spend more time with him.

MRS. JOYCE WOODWORTH

I was a teacher and then principal at Thomas Edison Elementary School in Daly City, CA. Later in my career I became the director of curriculum at the district office.

When I first met David, he was in my fifth grade reading class. I didn't hear about David before he was in my class because we only heard about students who had discipline problems, and he did not. David's appearance was unkempt and his shirt hung down over his fingertips because he had burns and scars. The other kids made fun of him, and he was always hungry and would steal food from the other kids' lunches.

The fourth grade teacher, Mrs. Konstan, talked to me about David. She said she was worried for his safety at home and was pushing to get help for Dave. We compiled three months of documentation to present to Child Protective Services. In those days the ruling belief was that the child was always better off with their biological family than being in foster care. One day, Dave arrived at school with his hands and the entire length of his arms burned from ammonia and Clorox, and that was the straw that broke the camel's back. I remember Mr. Hanson, the principal, calling and tearing into Child Protective Services about David, and how all the staff feared for him.

David's mother, Mrs. Pelzer, would come to the school to justify things that happened to David at home. When she came to the school she looked like the epitome of Mrs. PTA and a caring mother—plus she was a nurse—but I wasn't fooled. I knew better, and I called protective services.

I was home with the flu the day the police came to the school to take David directly to foster care. The principal called to inform me. The whole staff was so relieved that David was finally safe and away from his mother, but at the same time I was angered that it had taken the effort of so many people for so long in order to have Child Protective Services take action. I remember Mr. Ziegler doing so much to help. All of us did.

David would call me every time he was moved to a new foster home. He always wanted me to know where he was living.

On the twentieth anniversary of Dave's rescue, he presented me with a signed copy of his first book, *A Child Called "It."* I cried. I was overwhelmed and surprised that he took the bull by the horns and put in writing what had happened to him to help others.

I was present the day David was on *The Montel Williams Show* and then on *Oprah*. Both events were exciting. I was proud of David and felt it was about time he got the recognition he deserved for helping so many.

In the past when people have said malicious things about David and doubted his story, I always thought, "I was there. I know the truth, and I can speak the facts, and the facts are documented." It might be bizarre for people to believe, but I know it is true.

As an adult and after he wrote *A Child Called "It"* David would return to my school each year and talk with the students. The kids loved his sense of humor. It helped them receive his message. David went on to include the local junior high school for presentations, and each time he came we would meet and have lunch with him. One year I had a reception at my home for him, and I have a treasured photo of that time. It is a lovely memory.

For well over twenty years, David has given huge bouquets of flowers on Mother's Day to the teachers who saved him, and with the passing of Mrs. Konstan he continues the tradition by sending flowers to her daughter, Adrienne.

David's accomplishments are having the courage to make something of himself and his dedication to helping others. I would like to think that his foster parents had some role in helping David to have the courage to choose a different life. I would like the world to know there isn't a selfish bone in his body.

GEORGE SALLAS

If one were to look up the definition of someone who is socially conscious, the results would describe Dave Pelzer to a T. I have known Dave for fourteen years and have never known another person who is so generous with both his time and his fortune. I know the same can be said of a number of people, but rarely do we see a person that talks the talk *and* walks the walk. At the same time, Dave tends to shun the spotlight, seldom taking credit for his efforts. There are people who have known Dave for years but still have no idea of who he is or what he does. His early years and the trials he triumphed over, along with his experiences as an adult, have shaped the man I have come to know.

How, do you ask, do I come by this information? I have been there when Dave has returned from trips where he has counseled kids and adults that have been victims of all sorts of abuse. I have witnessed his return from trips overseas, visiting the troops. I was there when Dave returned and detailed the horrors of the aftermath of Hurricane Katrina. I have seen him have his downtime interrupted by an emergency phone call asking for help or advice. Yes, Dave is on call 24/7. And through it all, you will never hear Dave complain. He sees helping people as his lot, no, his duty in life.

Dave does not limit his generosity to his travels. I am reminded of an incident I felt privileged to see. I work at a cigar store Dave frequents during his downtime. We are not far from a Marine combat training center so we see quite a few young Marines in our store. On this particular day, Dave was in the store entertaining us with tales of derring-do when a young couple walked in. Dave immediately recognized the young man as a member of the Marine Corps. He approached the couple, introduced himself, and offered to buy the young man a cigar. Now Dave could have had me go into our humidor and get the Marine any old cigar. But he had discovered the couple were newlyweds. And so, as is typical of Dave, he had me open his personal locker, where he keeps some of the finest cigars made, and retrieved a very special and rare cigar. He presented it to the young man as a wedding gift and thanked him for his service. What others don't know is that Dave also slipped the man some money to have a very nice dinner with his new bride. They exchanged a few more pleasantries and Dave said his good-byes and left. The young Marine asked about Dave, wanting to know who this man was. When we told him about Dave's celebrity the couple was taken aback. The following day the young Marine and his new bride came into the store with an envelope for Dave. What was in the envelope,

I will never know, but I'm sure Dave still has it, along with countless others that will never be seen. These are the quiet things Dave does that no one will ever see or know about. But I know.

KATHRYN ESTEY, EXECUTIVE DIRECTOR

I am the executive director of D-Esprit, the office of Dave Pelzer. This role includes being Dave's consigliere, spiritual confessor, and his family all wrapped into one. I am "M," like in the James Bond movies that he loves so much.

How do I capture in words the essence of Dave Pelzer the man? Well, I'm going to try.

He is pure of heart with spirit that flows from his electric-blue eyes. His strong, dynamic energy and lightning-fast mind connect points of information that others could never even try to assimilate.

He is physically strong and quick, with an extrasensory ability to feel what is going on around him. Whether in a Humvee in the middle of Baghdad or a crowded restaurant, he is a master at discerning danger or possible danger and how to save people from harm.

He has divided mental compartments that open and close while receiving information. This allows him to focus on what he is doing in the moment, which usually is intense and creative and safeguards him from any mental stress.

What are the consequences for a middle-aged man who received only the briefest loving touch as a child from his mother before it was snatched away—what do you think this did to his ability to pick the right relationships in his life, whether personal or business or selecting a woman to be his mate? Or the consequences for a man who didn't have sisters, a man who comes from a childhood of trauma and abuse? His life since being rescued has been a process of learning how to be in respectful, loving, and secure relationships, and while learning how to do this himself he has taught others to do the same.

Because Dave always wanted a superhero (his dad) to rescue him, he has become a superhero to others. Day in and day out he helps people to climb out of the abyss of "nothingness" and to realize that they are resilient and can bounce back without rumination or regret. Dave helps people understand that when personal leadership and integrity is used in everyday life, it keeps you on a path you can live with and feel good about.

Dave loves life and believes he was blessed by being saved, and this led to his mission to help others feel better about themselves and move forward in life. This includes his volunteer time spent in places of war and disaster like Katrina, Joplin, Baghdad, Ramstein AFB in Germany, Bethesda, and military bases all over the country and overseas. When a military base is closing or military suicides are on the rise, Dave is the one who is called to come and assist. Dave stops his life and gets on a jet to attend to whatever base needs him with no thought or expectation of reimbursement. While reading this book you can see how the burning mission that drives him has also marked his career and personal life. The amount of work Dave does in a year's time to help others would make your head spin—he is like an action figure.

I don't want to forget to mention Dave's sense of humor. A real-life, A-list Hollywood action star once told Dave he was a cross between James Bond and Jack Bauer. Dave immediately quipped back in real life, saying, "No. I'm *soooo* Mr. Magoo." That's my Dave.

It is hard for Dave to give and receive love because it might be snatched away. His personal journey has been about discovering unconditional love, which is what I call love realized, and that makes Dave a living, breathing example of a resilient man who has done a step-by-step reconstruction of his life after experiencing a horrific childhood. He is a catalyst for social change. He values all life and he lives it every day.

ABOUT THE AUTHOR

A retired air force aircrew member, Dave played a major role in Operations Just Cause, Desert Shield, and Desert Storm. Dave was selected for the unique task of midair refueling of the once highly secretive SR-71 Blackbird and the F-117 Stealth Fighter. While serving in the air force, Dave worked in juvenile hall and other programs involving at-risk youth throughout California.

Dave's exceptional accomplishments include commendations from Presidents Ronald Reagan, George H. W. Bush, Bill Clinton, and George W. Bush, as well as other various heads of state. While maintaining an international active-duty flight schedule, Dave was the recipient of the 1990 J.C. Penney Golden Rule Award, making him the California Volunteer of the Year. In 1993, Dave was honored as one of the Ten Outstanding Young Americans (TOYA), joining a distinguished group of alumni that includes Chuck Yeager, Christopher Reeve, Anne Bancroft, John F. Kennedy, Orson Welles, and Walt Disney. In 1994, Dave was the only American to be selected as one of The Outstanding Young Persons of the World (TOYP) for his efforts involving child abuse awareness and prevention, as well as for instilling resilience and self-responsibility in others. During the Centennial Olympic Games, Dave was a torchbearer, carrying the coveted flame. Dave is also the recipient of the 2005 National Jefferson Award, which is considered the Pulitzer Prize for public service. Other recipients include Sandra Day O'Connor and former secretary of state Colin Powell.

Dave is the author of seven other inspirational books including *A Child Called "It,"* which has been on the *New York Times* best-seller list for more than six years. All combined, his books have been on the *New York Times* best-seller list for well over thirteen years. He is one of the only authors to have four #1 international best sellers, and to have four books simultaneously on the *New York Times* best-seller list.

When not on the road, spending time with his son, Stephen, or serving his community as a certified volunteer firefighter, Dave lives a quiet life in Northern California with his wife, Kathy, and their demanding diva cat, the infamous El Gato.

Dave is a living testament to resilience, faith in humanity, and personal responsibility. Dave's unique and inspirational outlook on life, coupled with his sense of humor, entertains and encourages others to overcome their obstacles while living life to its fullest.

Dave also provides specific programs to those who work in the human service and educational fields as well as giving a specific presentation about writing and the inner workings of the publishing field.

For additional information on having Dave for your group, you can call or visit his website:

Phone: 760-321-0364
www.davepelzer.com